RECORDED VERSIONS GUITAR

AUTHENTIC TRANSCRIPTIONS
WITH NOTES AND TABLATURE

O, YEAH!

ULTIMATE AEROSMITH HITS

ISBN 978-0-634-05674-1

HAL•LEONARD® CORPORATION

7777 W. BLUEMOUND RD. P.O. BOX 13819 MILWAUKEE, WI 53213

Visit Hal Leonard Online at
www.halleonard.com

Contents

Mama Kin

Words and Music by Tyler

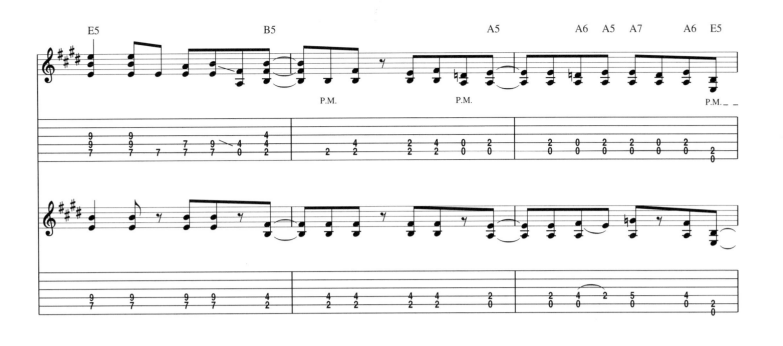

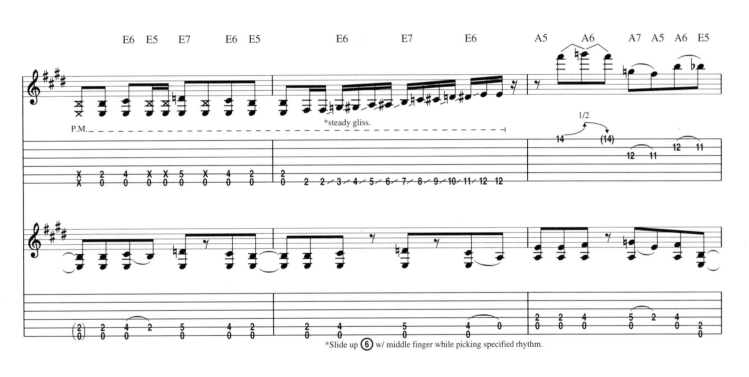

*Slide up ⑥ w/ middle finger while picking specified rhythm.

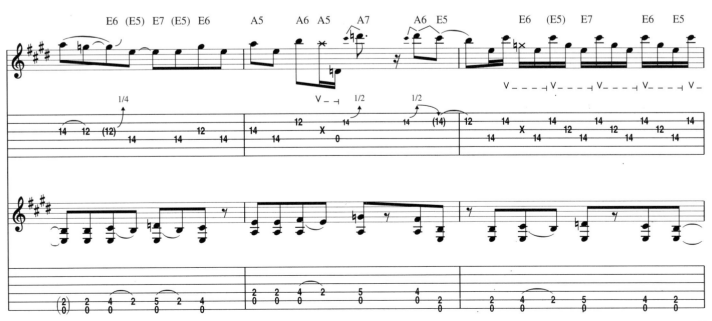

6

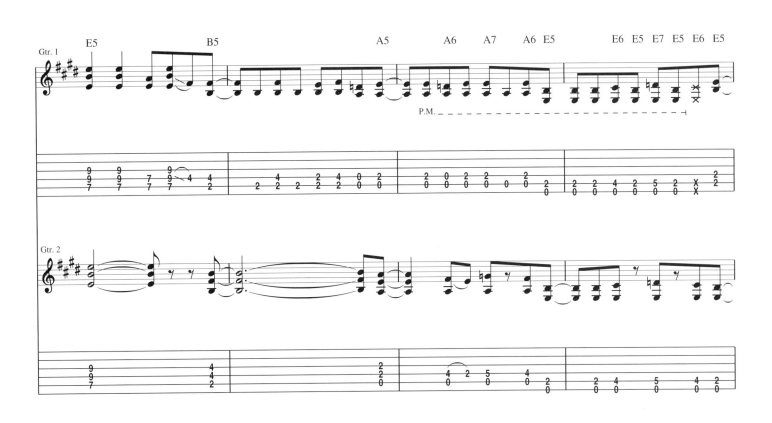

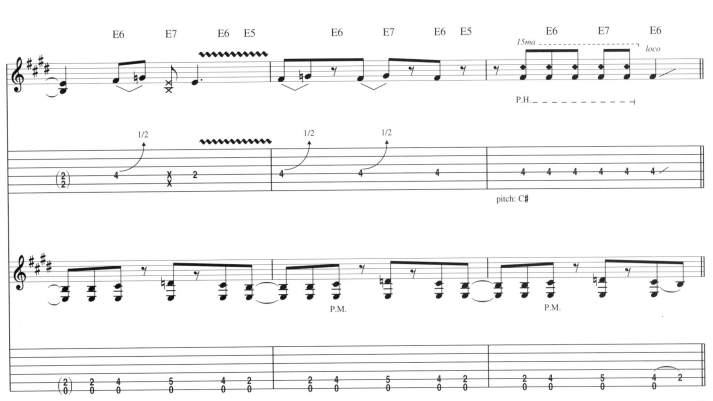

Whole-earth lov-er, keep-in' un-der-cov-er, ___ nev-

-er know-in' where ya been. ___

You've been fad-in', al-ways out par-ad-in'. ___ Keep ___ in touch with ma-ma kin.

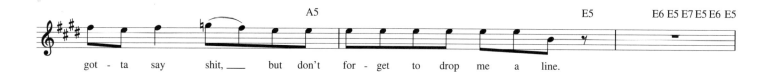

got - ta say shit, ___ but don't for - get to drop me a line.

Pre-Chorus

Gtrs. 1 & 2: w/ Rhy. Figs. 2 & 2A, simile

Said, ___ you're as bald as an egg at eigh - teen, ___ an' work - in' for your dad is just a ___

___ drag. ___ He still stuff your mouth with your dream. ___

You bet - ter check it out, 'cause some - day soon you'll have ta climb back on the

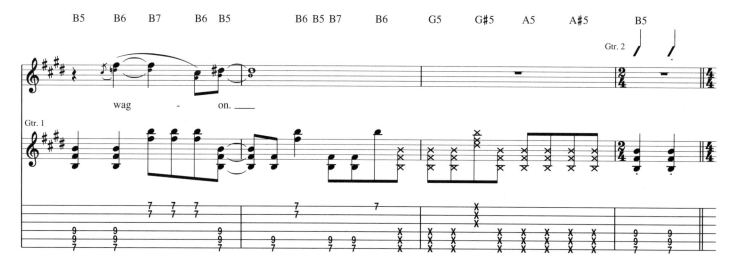

wag - on. ___

Gtr. 1

Chorus

Gtr. 2 tacet

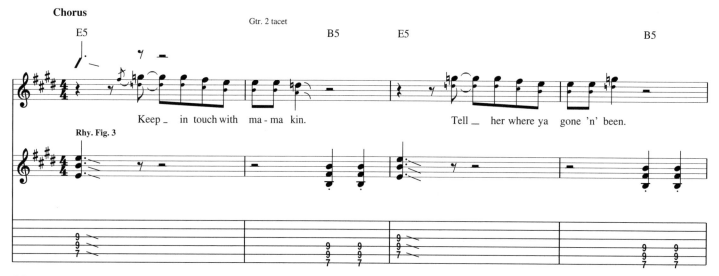

Keep ___ in touch with ma - ma kin. Tell ___ her where ya gone 'n' been.

Rhy. Fig. 3

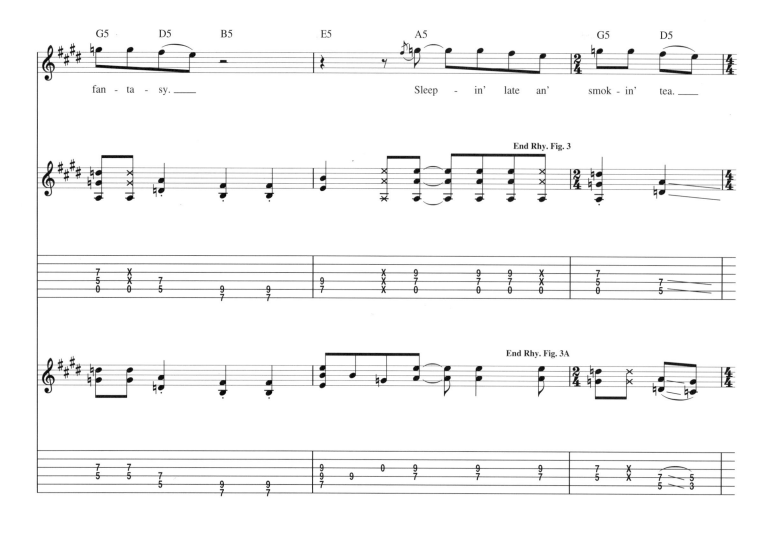

fan - ta - sy. _____ Sleep - in' late an' smok - in' tea. _____

End Rhy. Fig. 3

End Rhy. Fig. 3A

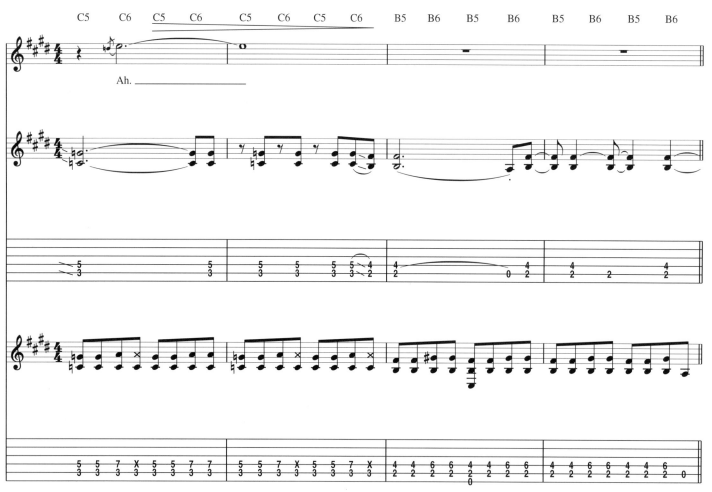

Ah. _____

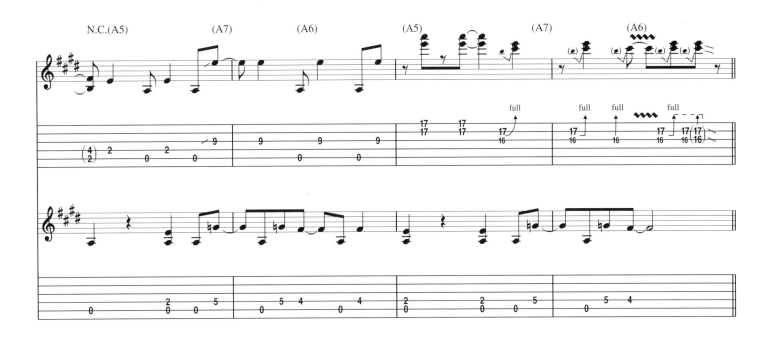

Verse

Gtrs. 1 & 2: w/ Rhy. Figs. 1 & 1A, simile

E5   B5   A5   E5   E6 E7 E6 E5

3. It ain't eas-y, liv-in' like you wan-na. And it's ___ so hard ta find peace of mind. ___ Yes, it

E6   E7   E6   E5   B5   A5   E5

is.   The way I see it, you got-ta say shit, ___ but don't for-get to drop me a line.

Pre-Chorus

Gtr. 1: w/ Rhy. Fig. 2, 1st 7 meas., simile
Gtr. 2: w/ Rhy. Fig. 2A, 1st 4 meas., simile

E6 E7 E6 E5   E6 E7   E6   A5 A6 A5 A7 A5 A6 E5   E6 E5 E7 E5 E6   A5   A6 A5 A7 A5 A6 E5

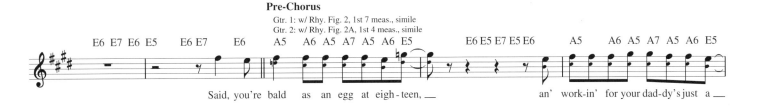

Said, you're bald as an egg at eigh-teen, ___   an' work-in' for your dad-dy's just a ___

Gtr. 2: w/ Rhy. Fill 1   Gtr. 2: w/ Rhy. Fig. 2A, last 7 meas. simile

E6 E5 E7 E5 E6   E5   E6 E5 E7 E5 E6   A5   A6 A5 A7 A5 A6 E5   E6 E5 E7 E5 E6

___ drag. ___   He still stuffs your mouth with your dreams. .   You

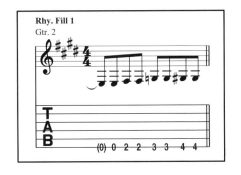

ma - ma kin. ____ I said, a - tell her where ya gone 'n' been.

Liv - in' out your fan - ta - sy. ____ Sleep - in' late an'

smok - in' tea. ____

Gtr. 1

Gtr. 2

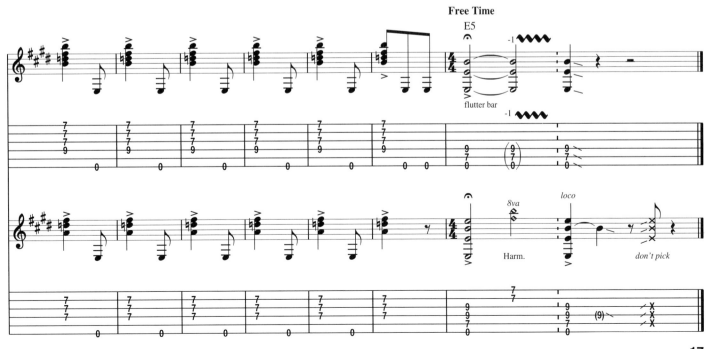

Dream On

Words and Music by Tyler

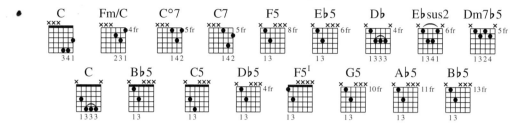

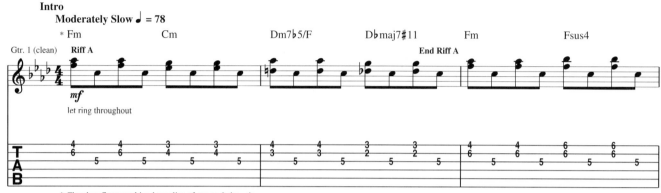

Intro

Moderately Slow ♩ = 78

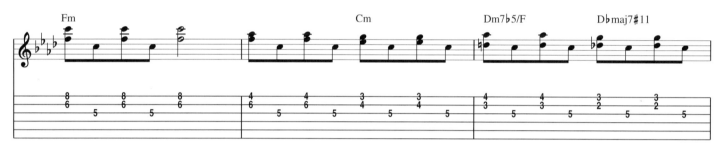

let ring throughout

* Chords reflect combined tonality of gtr. and elec. piano.

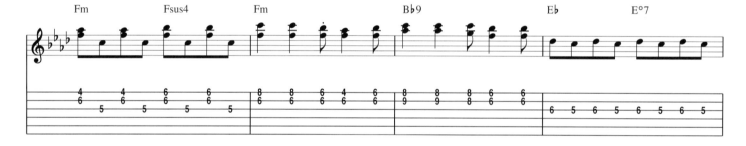

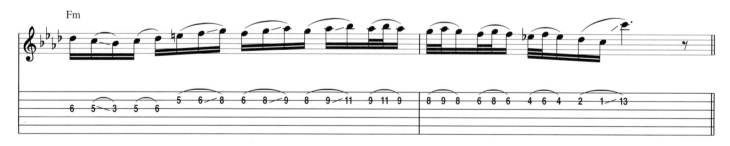

Verse

Gtr. 1: w/ Riff A, 4 times

1. Ev-'ry time ___ that I look in the mir - ror, all these lines ___ in my face get-tin' clear - er.

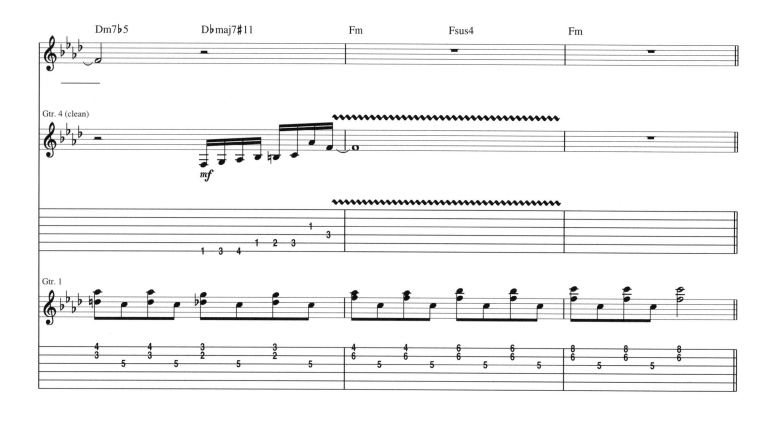

Verse

Gtr. 4 tacet
Gtr. 1: w/ Riff A, 4 times

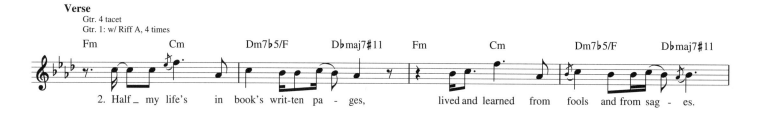

2. Half _ my life's in book's writ-ten pa - ges, lived and learned from fools and from sag - es.

You know _ it's true _____ all these things _____ come back to you. _____

% Pre-Chorus

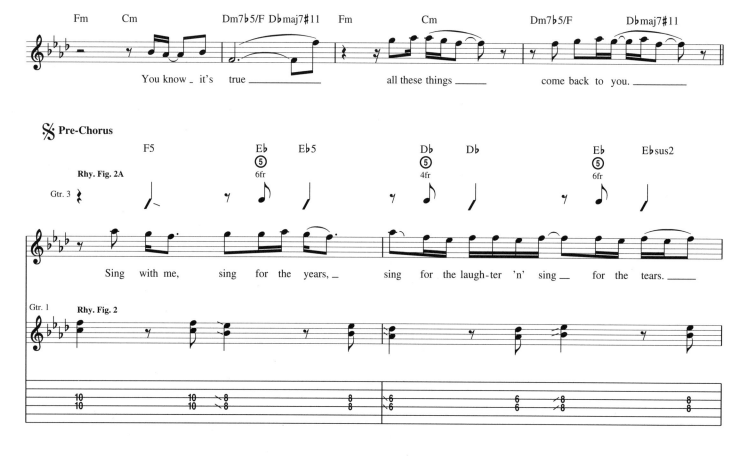

Sing with me, sing for the years, _ sing for the laugh-ter 'n' sing _ for the tears. ____

Sing _ with me if it's just for to - day, _ may-be to - mor - row the good Lord will take you a - way. _

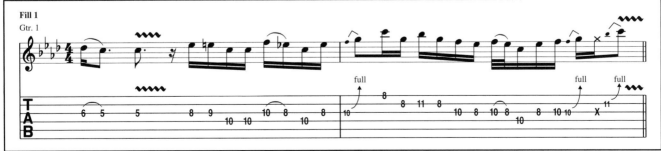

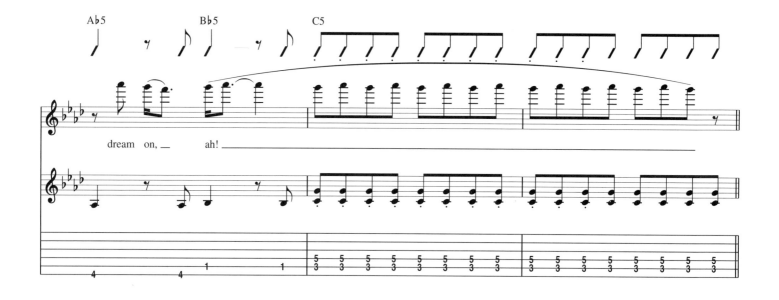

dream on, __ ah! _____

Pre-Chorus

Gtrs. 1 & 3: w/ Rhy. Figs. 1 & 1A

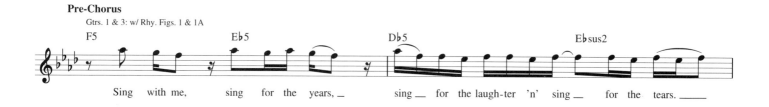

Sing with me, sing for the years, __ sing __ for the laugh-ter 'n' sing __ for the tears. ____

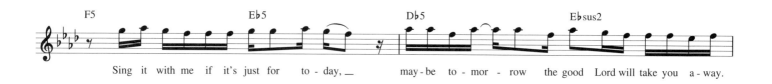

Sing it with me if it's just for to-day, __ may-be to-mor-row the good Lord will take you a-way.

Gtrs. 1 & 3: w/ Rhy. Figs. 2 & 2A

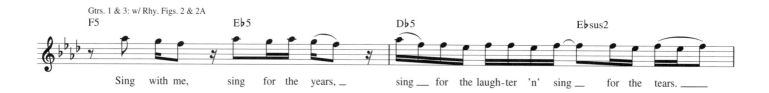

Sing with me, sing for the years, __ sing __ for the laugh-ter 'n' sing __ for the tears. ____

Gtr. 4: w/ Riff B

Sing it with me if it's just for to-day, __ may-be to-mor-row the good Lord will take you a-way. __

Outro

Gtrs. 1, 3 & 4 tacet

Gtr. 2

Repeat and Fade

N.C.(C5)

let ring ____

Same Old Song & Dance

Words and Music by Tyler/Perry

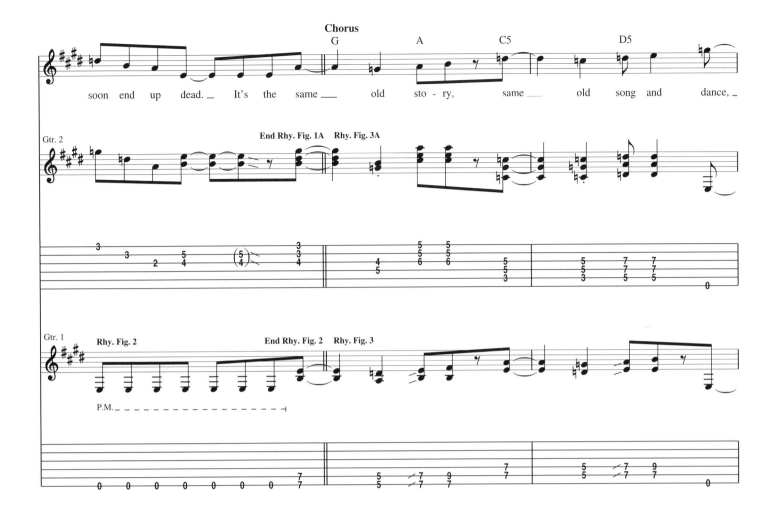

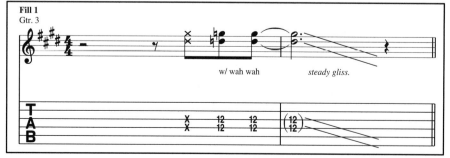

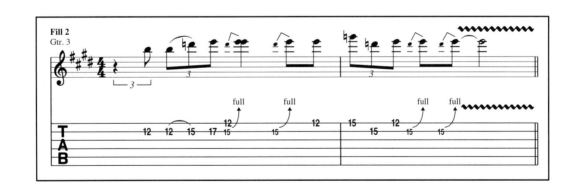

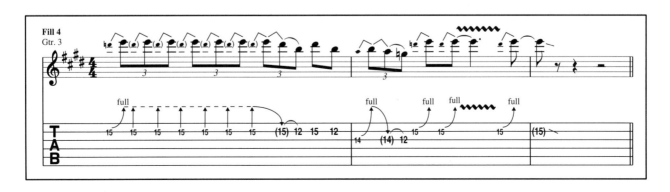

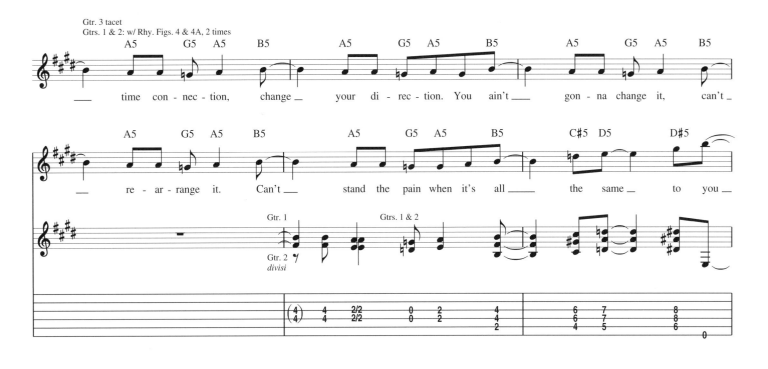

time con - nec - tion, change your di - rec - tion. You ain't gon - na change it, can't

re - ar - range it. Can't stand the pain when it's all the same to you

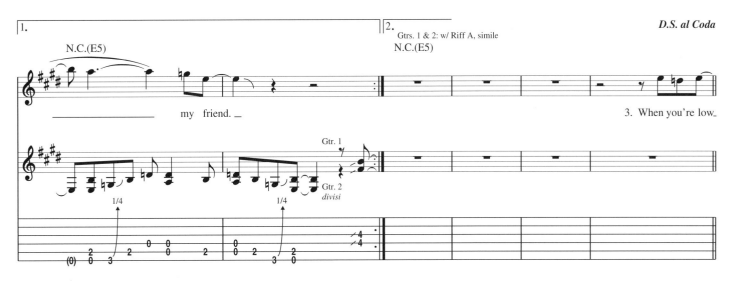

1.

N.C.(E5)

my friend.

2. Gtrs. 1 & 2: w/ Riff A, simile

N.C.(E5)

D.S. al Coda

3. When you're low

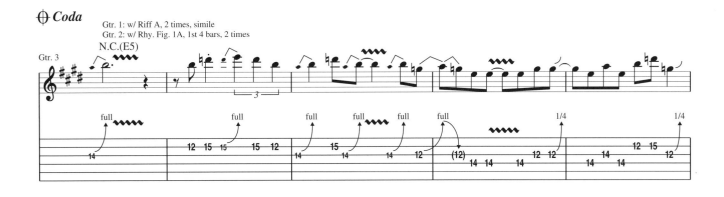

Coda

Gtr. 1: w/ Riff A, 2 times, simile
Gtr. 2: w/ Rhy. Fig. 1A, 1st 4 bars, 2 times

Gtr. 3

N.C.(E5)

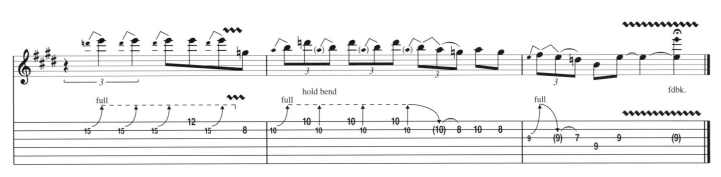

Seasons of Wither

Words and Music by Tyler

Gtrs. 4 & 6: Drop D tuning:
(low to high) D-A-D-G-B-E

Intro

Moderately slow Rock ♩ = 97

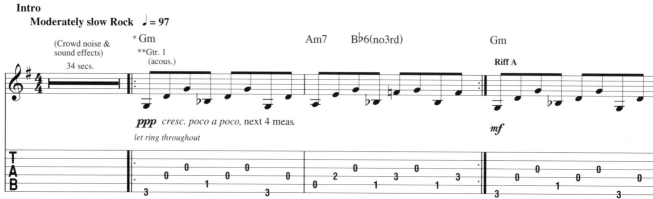

*Chord symbols reflect implied harmony.

**Doubled throughout

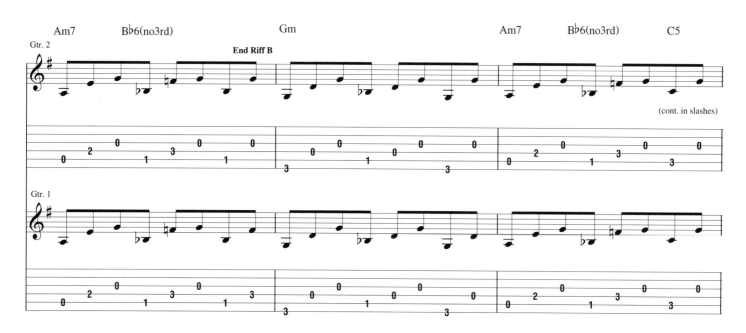

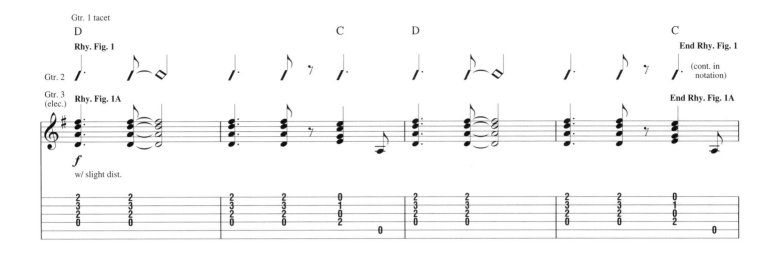

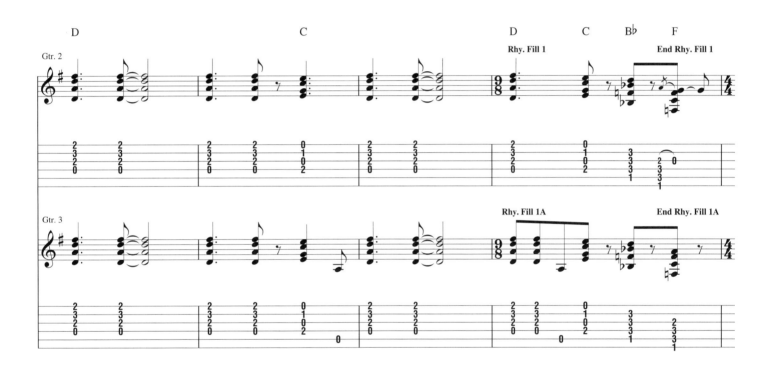

*Gtr. 3 *let ring throughout*

Verse

Gtrs. 1 & 3: w/ Riff C (3 3/4 times)
Gtr. 2: w/ Riff C1 (3 3/4 times)

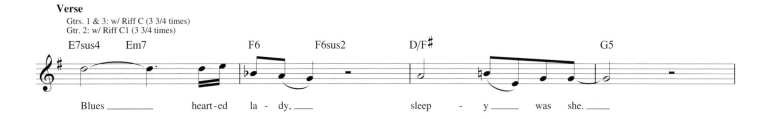

Blues _____ heart-ed la - dy, _____ sleep - y _____ was she. _____

Love _____ for the dev - il _____ brought her _____ to me. _____

Seas _____ of a thou - sand _____ drawn to _____ her sin. _____

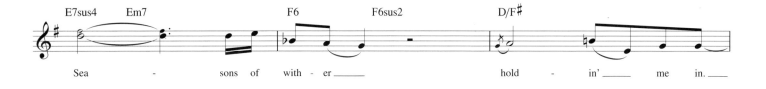

Sea - sons of with - er _____ hold - in' _____ me in. _____

𝄋 Chorus

Ooh, _____ woe is me. _____ I feel _ so bad -

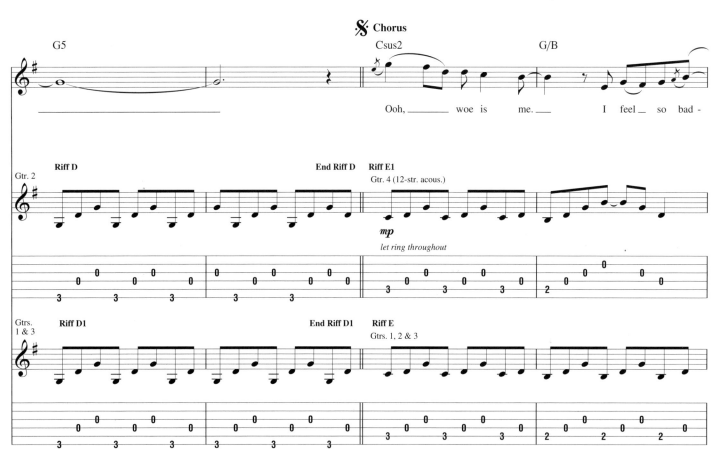

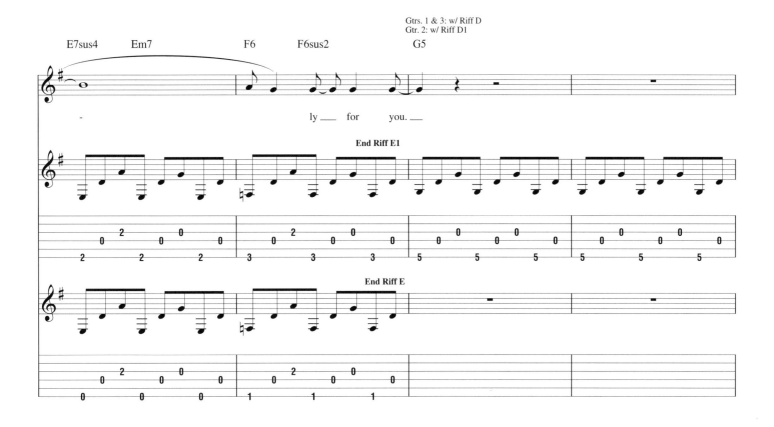

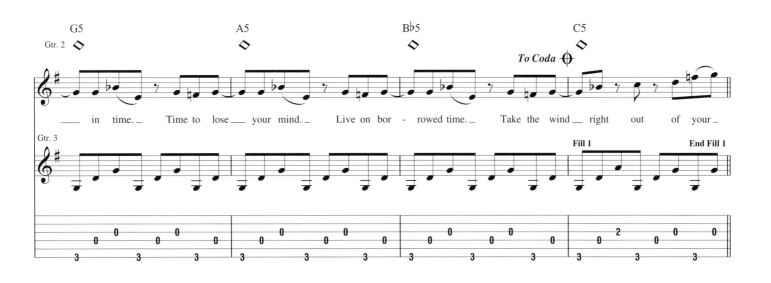

Bridge

Fire - flies ___ dance ___ in the heat ___ of ___ hound dogs ___ that bay ___

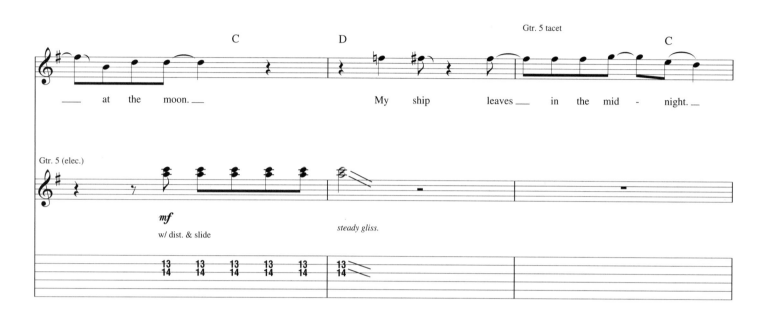

___ at the moon. ___   My ship leaves ___ in the mid - night. ___

mf

w/ dist. & slide   *steady gliss.*

Verse

Can't say I'll ___ be back too ___ soon. ___   2. They a -

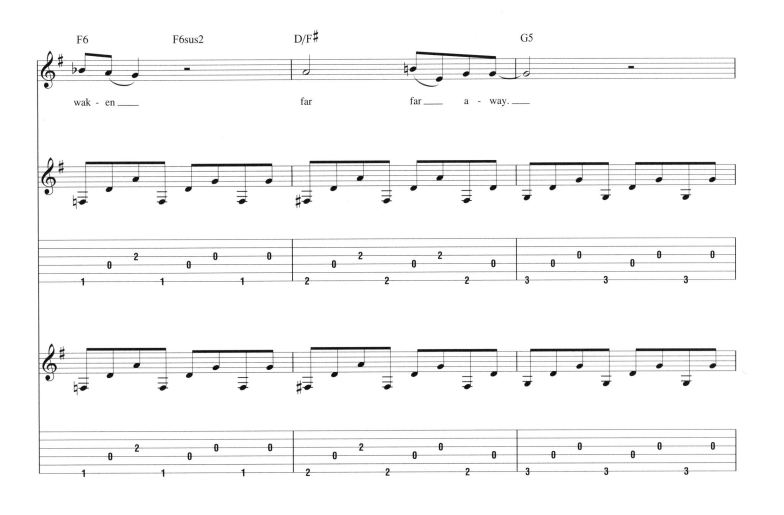

wak - en ___ far far ___ a - way. ___

Gtrs. 1 & 3: w/ Riff C (2 3/4 times)
Gtr. 2: w/ Riff C1 (2 3/4 times)

E7sus4 Em7   F6   F6sus2   D/F#   G5

Heat ___ of my can - dle ___ show me ___ the way. ___

E7sus4 Em7   F6   F6sus2   D/F#   G5

Seas ___ of a thou - sand ___ drawn to ___ her sin. ___

D.S. al Coda

Gtrs. 1 & 3: w/ Riff D
Gtr. 2: w/ Riff D1

E7sus4 Em7   F6   F6sus2   D/F#   G5

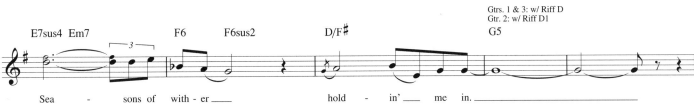

Sea - sons of with - er ___ hold - in' me in. ___

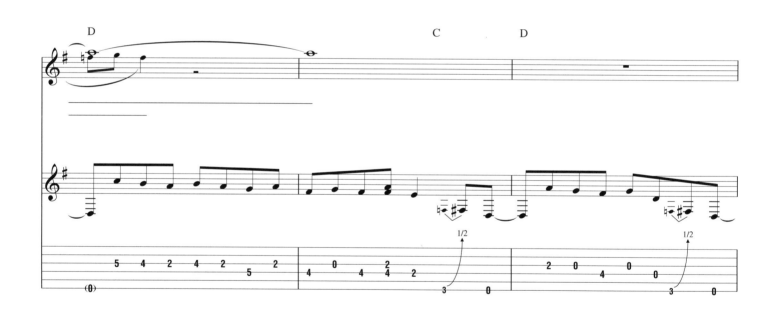

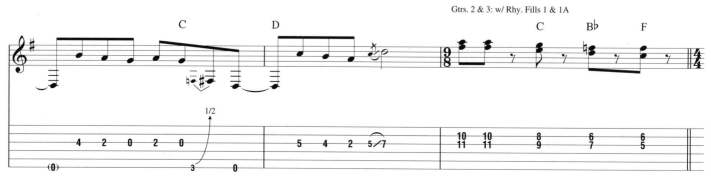

Outro - Guitar Solo

Gtrs. 2 & 3: w/ Riffs C & C1 (1st 3 meas.)   Gtr. 6 tacet

Gtrs. 1 & 3: w/ Riff A (3 1/2 times)
Gtr. 2: w/ Riff B1 (3 1/2 times)

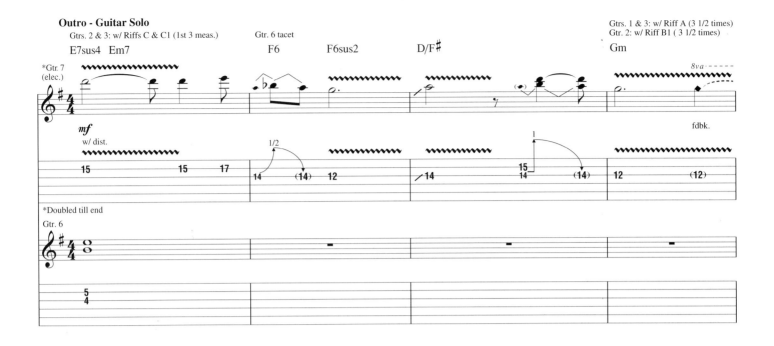

*Doubled till end

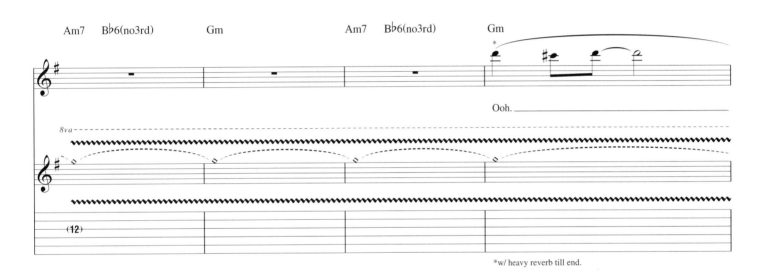

*w/ heavy reverb till end.

Fade out

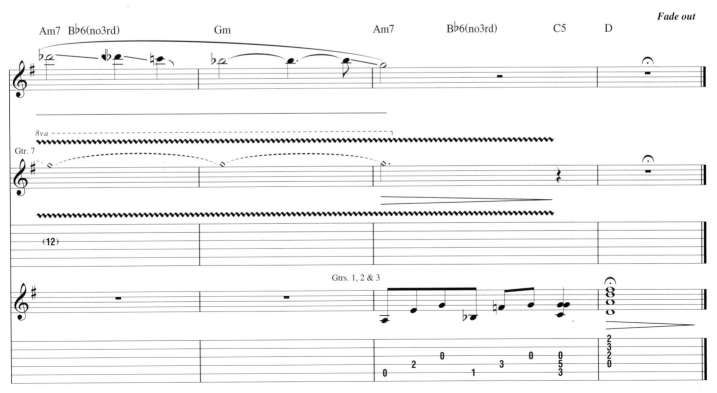

Gtrs. 1, 2 & 3

Walk This Way

Words and Music by Tyler/Perry

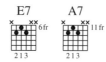

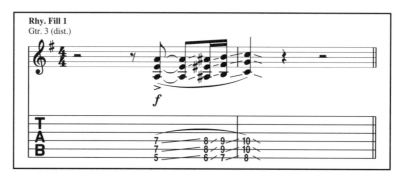

ain't   seen   noth-in'   till   you're   down   on   a   muf-fin   and   you're   sure   to   be   a-chang-in'   your   ways."   I   met   a
three   young   la-dies   in   the   school   gym   lock-er   when   I   no-ticed   they   was   look-in'   at   me.   I   was   a

P.M.

Gtr. 3: w/ Rhy. Fill 2, 2nd time

cheer   -   lead-er,   was   a   real   young   bleed-er   all   the   times   I   could   rem   -   i   -   nisce,   'cause   the
high   school   los-er,   nev-er   made   it   with   a   la-dy   'til   the   boys   told   me   some-thin'   I   missed,   then   my

Rhy. Fig. 2

P.M.

A5

best   things   in   lov-in'   with   a   sis-ter   and   a   cou-sin   on-ly   start-ed   with   a   lit-tle   kiss,   a-like   this!
next   door   neigh-bor   with   a   daugh-ter   had   a   fav-or   so   I   gave   her   just   a   lit-tle   kiss   a-like   this!

End Rhy. Fig. 2

P.M.

f

Rhy. Fill 2
Gtr. 3

Interlude

Gtr. 1: w/ Riff A, 2nd time

N.C.(E5)

Gtr. 1

Gtr. 2
divisi

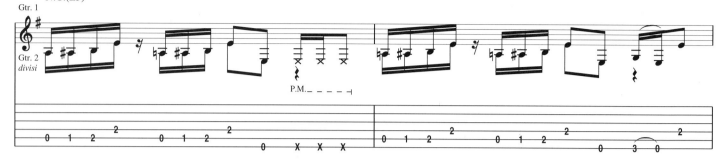

Gtr. 3: w/ Rhy. Fill 1

Gtrs. 1 & 2

A5

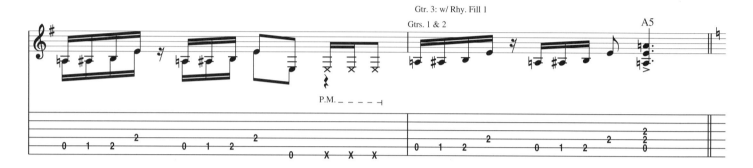

Verse

Gtrs. 1 & 2: w/ Rhy. Fig. 1, 3 times, simile

N.C.(C7)

2., 4. See - saw swing - in' with the boys in the school and your feet fly - in' up in the air, ___ I sing,

"Hey did - dle did - dle" with your kit - ty in the mid - dle of the swing like you did - n't care. __ So I

took a big chance at the high school dance with a miss - y who was read - y to play, __ was a

* Sing harmony 1st time only.

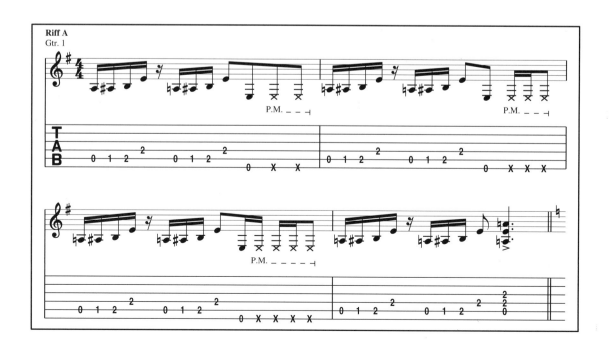

42

Guitar Solo

Gtrs. 1 & 2: w/ Rhy. Fig. 2

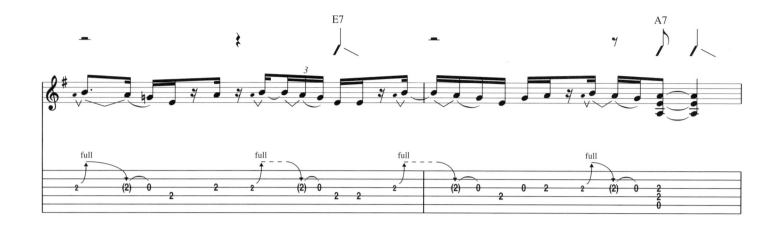

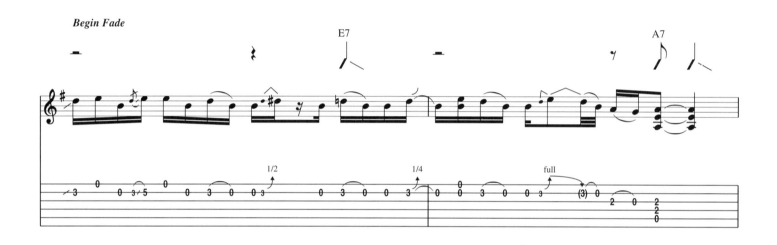

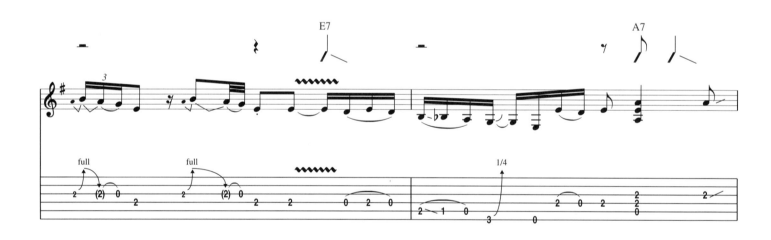

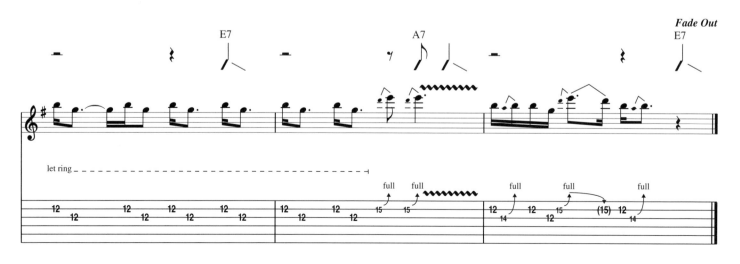

Big Ten Inch Record

Words and Music by Fred Weismantel

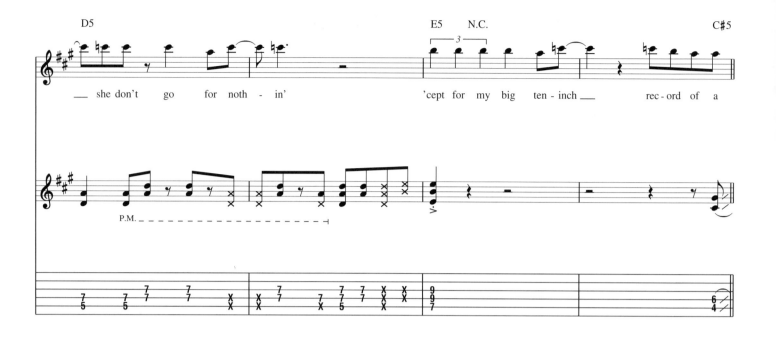

she don't go for noth - in'   'cept for my big ten - inch ___ rec - ord of a

Chorus

Gtr. 1: w/ Rhy. Fig. 2, 1st 5 meas., simile

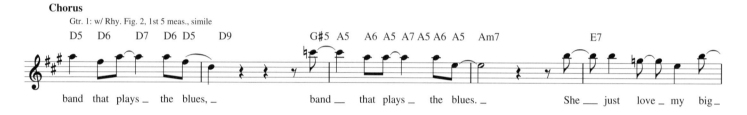

band that plays ___ the blues, ___ band ___ that plays ___ the blues. ___ She ___ just love ___ my big ___

Outro

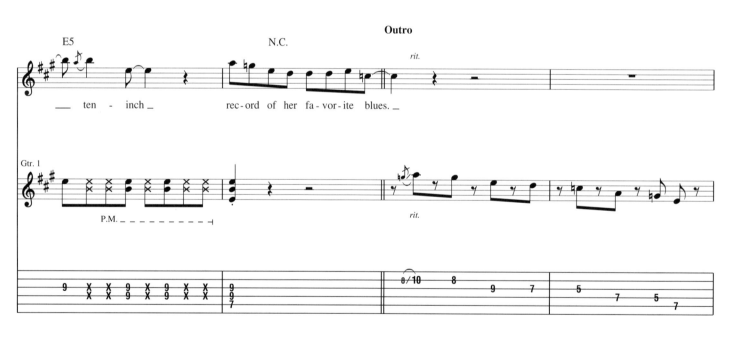

___ ten - inch ___ rec - ord of her fa - vor - ite blues. ___

Free Time

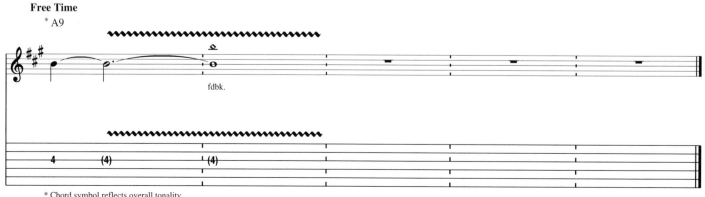

fdbk.

* Chord symbol reflects overall tonality.

Sweet Emotion

Words and Music by Tyler/Hamilton

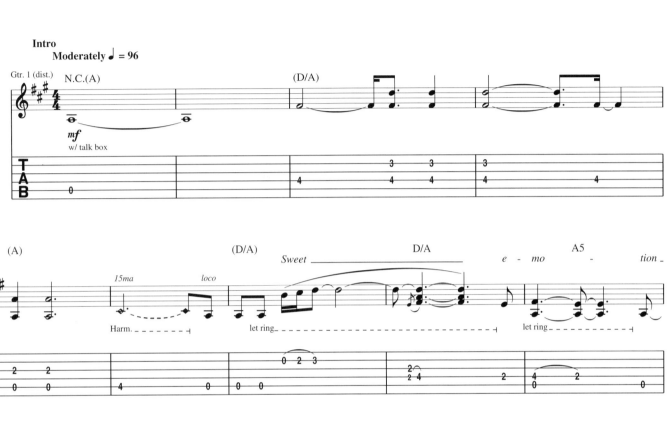

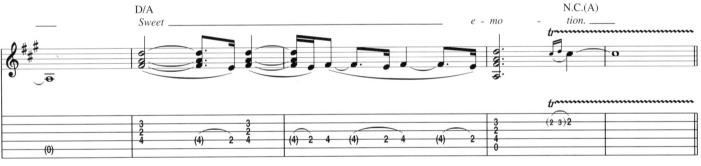

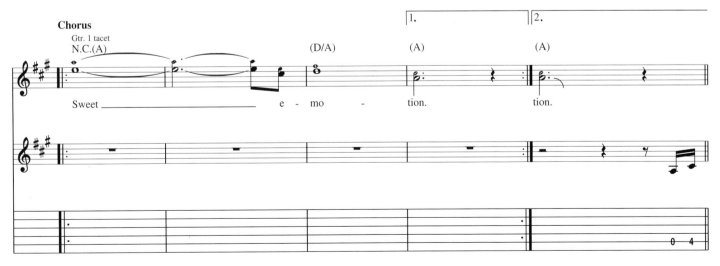

Last Child

Words and Music by Tyler/Whitford

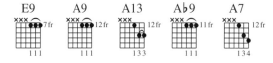

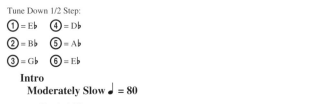

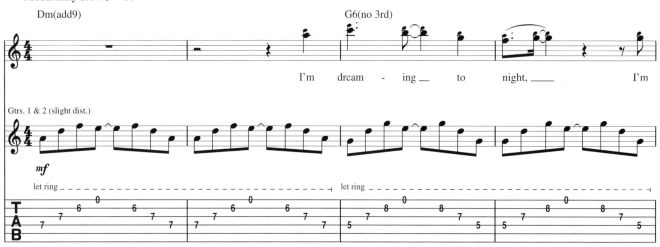

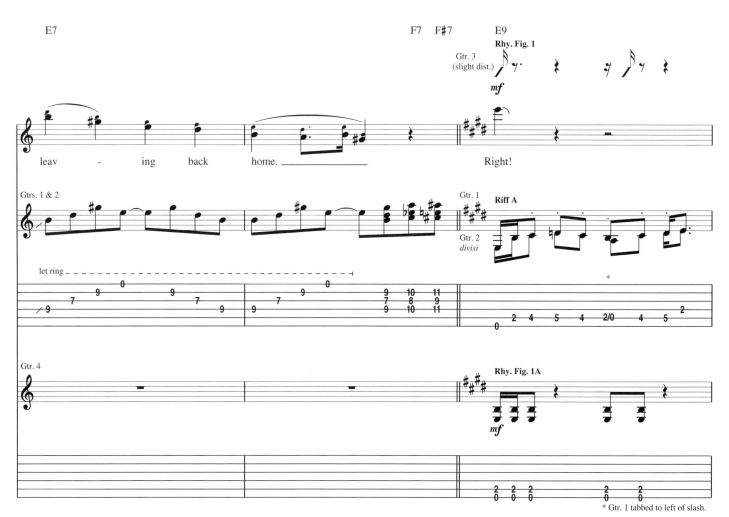

* Gtr. 1 tabbed to left of slash.

* Gtr. 4 tabbed to the right of slash.

tail poon - tang sweet - heart sweat who could make ___ silk purse from a J. Paul Get and his ear, ___
their throats for pap - er notes and their ba - bies cry while cit - ies lie at their feet, ___

*A7, 2nd time

with her face in her beer. ___
when you're rock-in' the streets. ___

Gtr. 1

Gtr. 2

Gtr. 4

Home   sweet

home.   2. Get out

Back in the Saddle

Words and Music by Tyler/Perry

look-in' for old Su - kie Jones, __ she cra-zy horse __ sa - loon. _____

Bar-keep gim-me a drink, _____ that's when she caught __ my eye, __ she

turned to gim-me a wink, _____ that'd make a grown __ man cry. _____ I'm

* Chord symbols reflect combined tonality

I scream for more.   Fools gold   out of their mine, _____

the girls are soak-in' wet. _   No tongue's dri-er than mine, _   I'll come when I   get

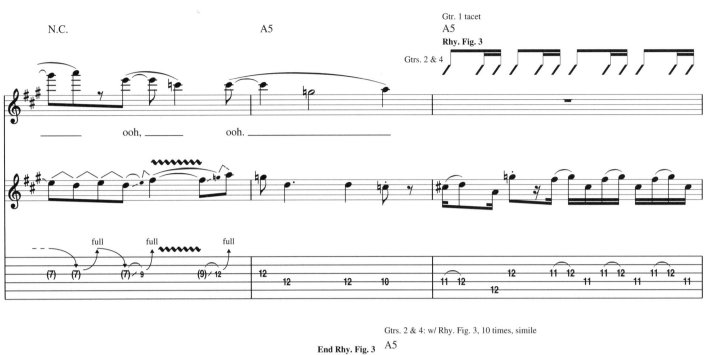

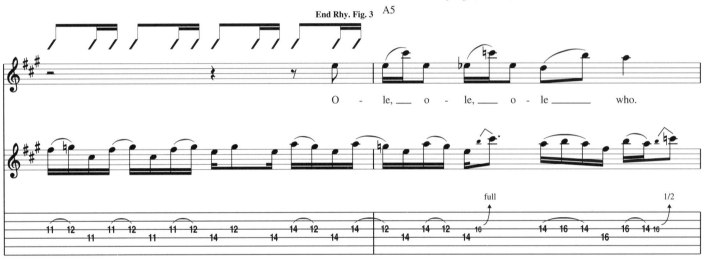

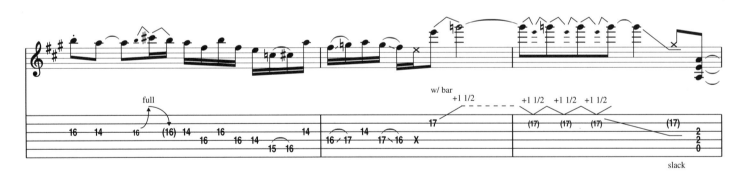

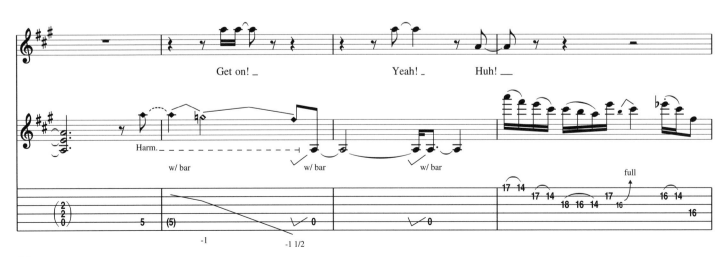

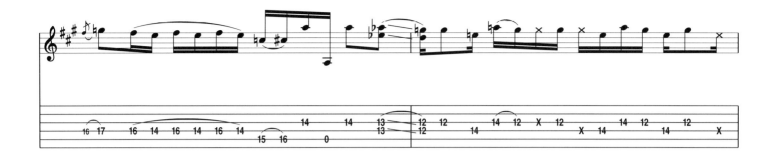

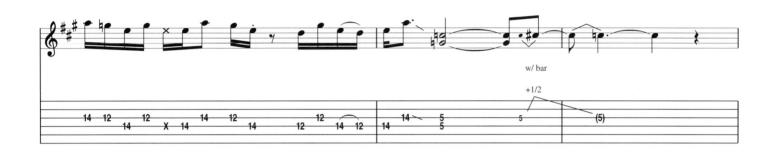

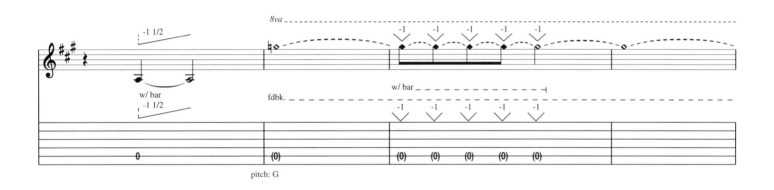

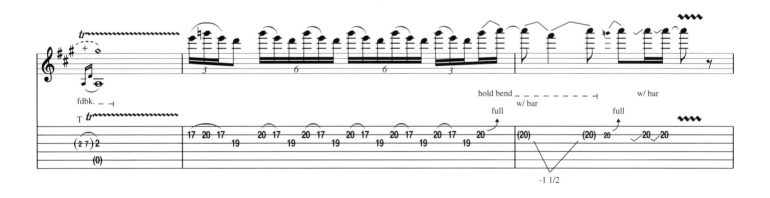

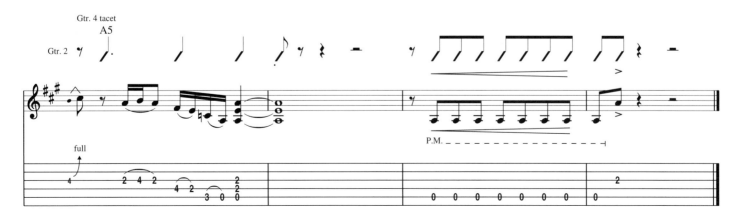

Draw the Line

Words and Music by Tyler/Perry

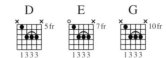

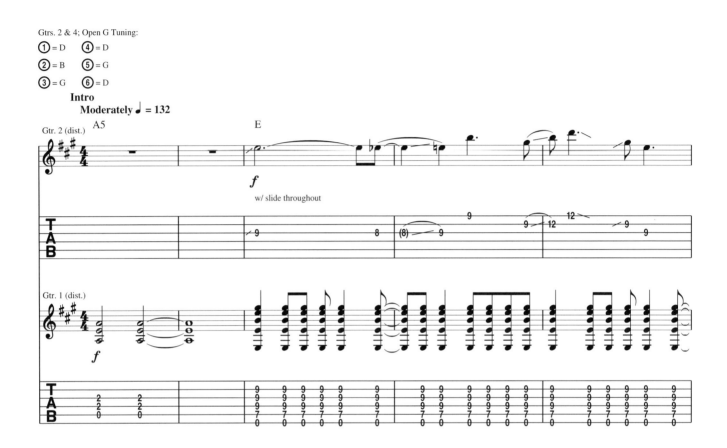

Verse

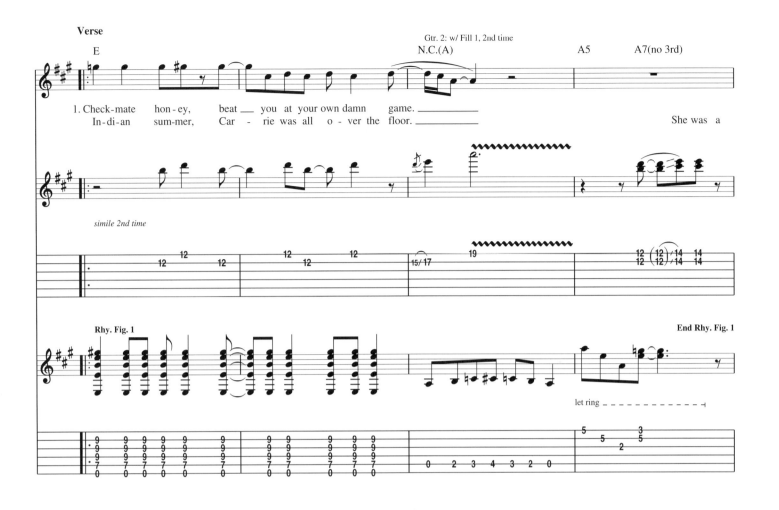

simile 2nd time

Rhy. Fig. 1

End Rhy. Fig. 1

let ring _ _ _ _ _ _ _ _

1. Check-mate hon-ey, beat __ you at your own damn game. __ She was a
   In-di-an sum-mer, Car-rie was all o-ver the floor. __

Gtr. 1: w/ Rhy. Fig. 1

No dice hon-ey, I'm liv-in' on the as-tral plane. __ Feet's __
wet net win-ner and rare-ly ev-er left the store. __ She'd sing and

Gtr. 2

Fill 1

Gtr. 2

steady gliss.

Check - mate hon - ey, you the on - ly one who's got to choose.

when to draw the line.

Gtr. 2

* Slide bar is off end of fingerboard at an imaginary 26th fret.

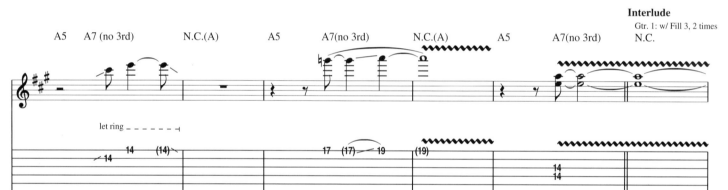

Interlude

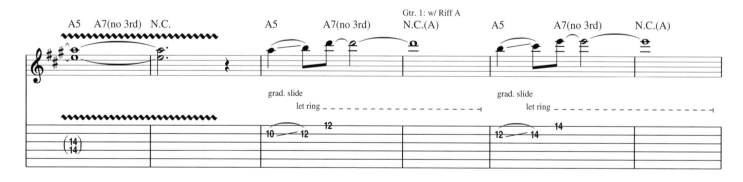

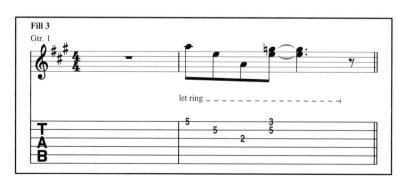

Gtr. 1: w/ Fill 4, 4 times
Gtr. 2 tacet

A5   A7(no 3rd)   N.C.(A)   A7(no 3rd)

Hon - ey,

Gtr. 3 (slight dist.)

mf
let ring

Bridge

Gtr. 3 tacet
E
Gtr. 1

let's check - mate, don't be late.   Take an - oth - er bow.   You say   you   cry ___ so far a - way and if you

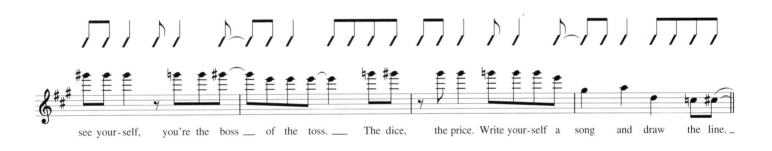

see your - self,   you're the boss ___ of the toss. ___   The dice,   the price. Write your - self a   song   and draw   the line. __

Outro

Gtr. 1: w/ Riff A, 8 times
Gtr. 4: w/ Fill 5, 8 times

N.C.(A)   A5   A7(no 3rd)   N.C.(A)   A5   A7(no 3rd)

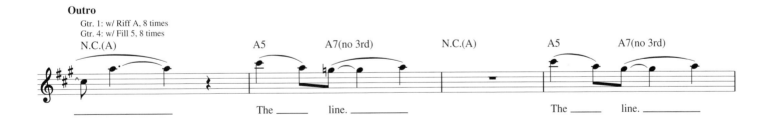

_____   The ___ line. _____   The ___ line. _____

Fill 4
Gtr. 1

Fill 5
Gtr. 4 (dist.)

mf w/ slide

Dude (Looks Like a Lady)

Words and Music by Tyler/Perry/Child

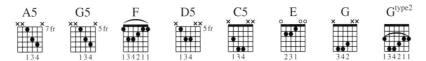

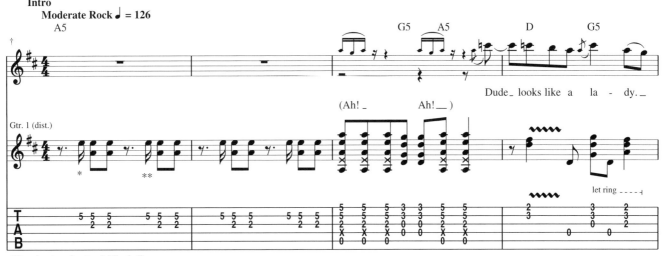

†Key signature denotes A Mixolydian.
*Panned hard left
**Panned hard right

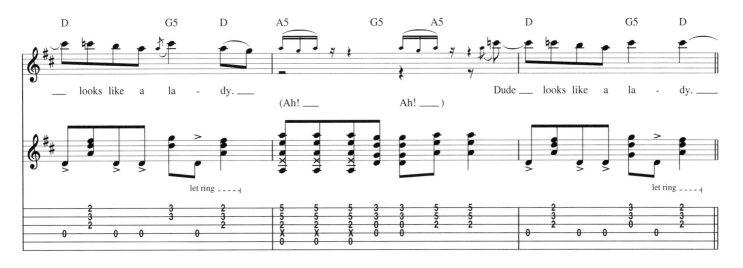

*Vocal tacet on repeat.

1. Cruised in-to a bar on the shore. _____ Her
2. Back-stage we're hav-ing the time _____ of our lives _____
never judge a book by it's cov-er _____ or

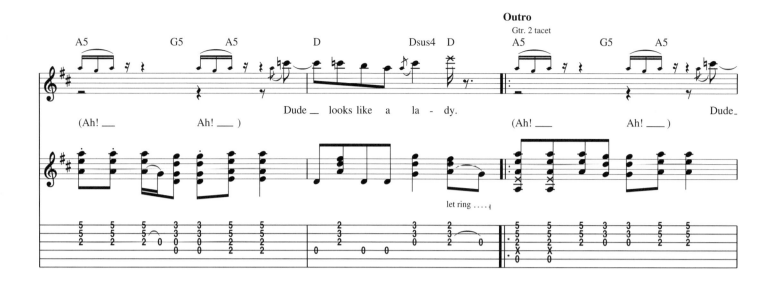

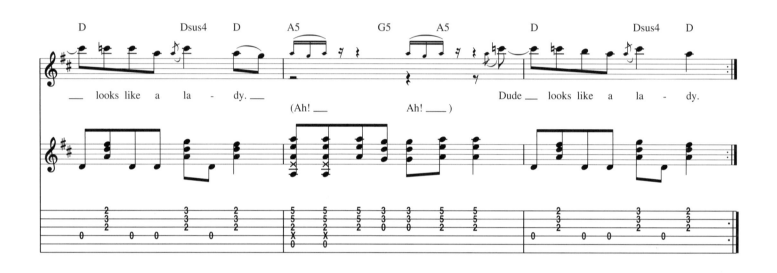

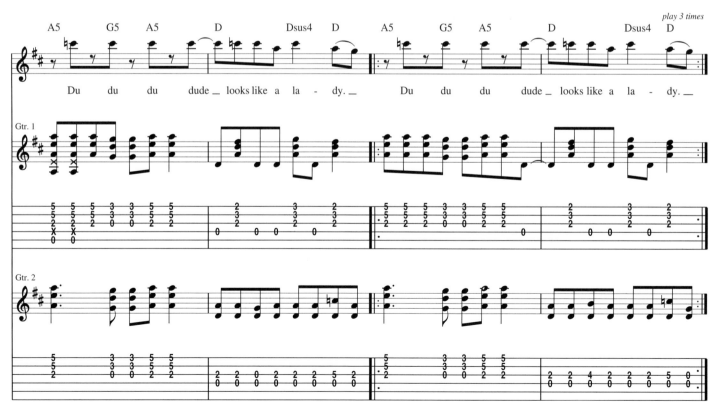

Angel

Words and Music by Tyler/Child

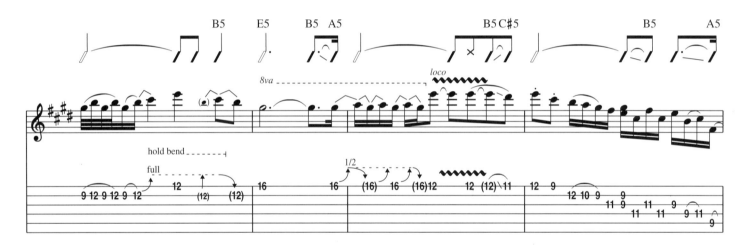

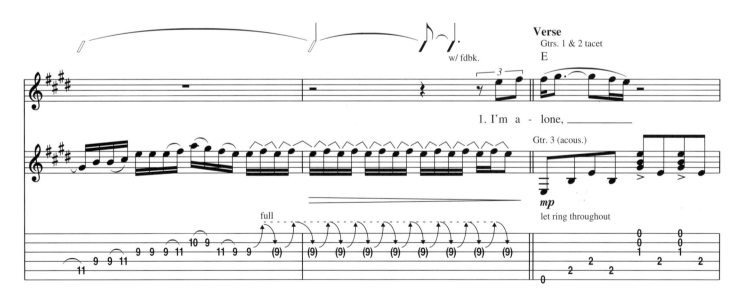

End Rhy. Fig. 1

C#5   B5   A5   B5   E5   B5 A5   B5

night. _____ You're my an - gel, ___ come and make it al -

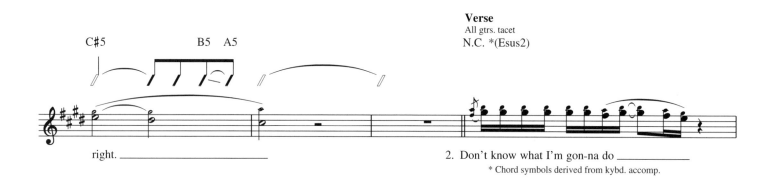

Verse
All gtrs. tacet
N.C. *(Esus2)

C#5   B5   A5

right. _____ 2. Don't know what I'm gon-na do _____

* Chord symbols derived from kybd. accomp.

(A)   (Asus4)   (A)   (Esus2)

a - bout _ this feel - in' in - side. ____ Yes, it's __ true _____

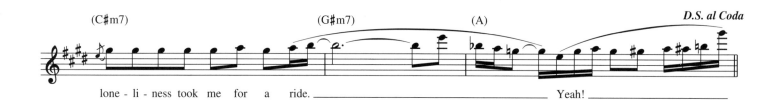

(C#m7)   (G#m7)   (A)   ***D.S. al Coda***

lone - li - ness took me for a ride. _____ Yeah!

⊕ *Coda 1*

Guitar Solo

C#5   B5   A5   B5   E5   B5   A5

Gtr. 1

right.   Come and save me to - night.

Gtr. 3

mf
w/ slight dist.

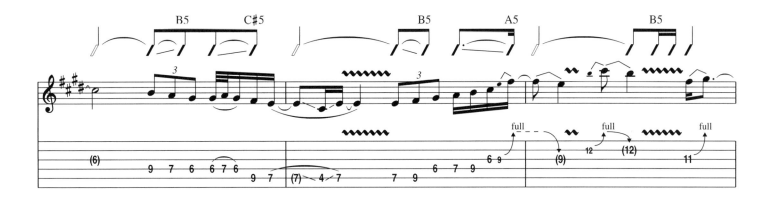

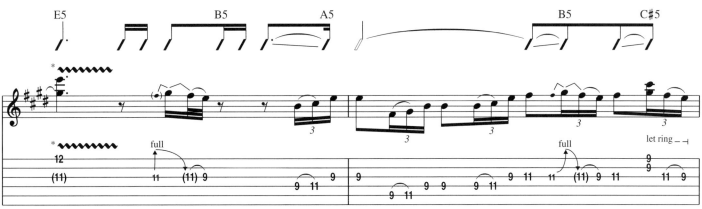

* Vib. applies to bent note only.

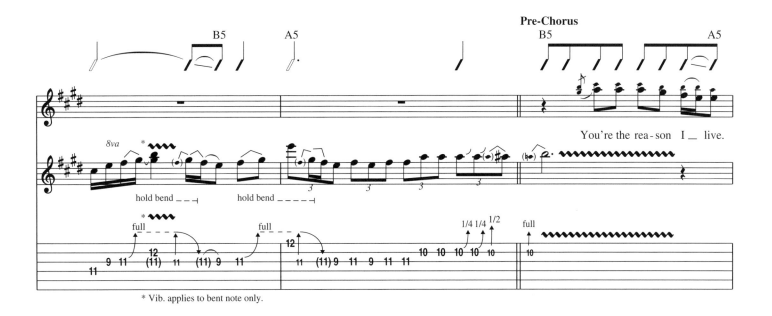

* Vib. applies to bent note only.

Rag Doll

Words and Music by Tyler/Perry/Knight/Vallance

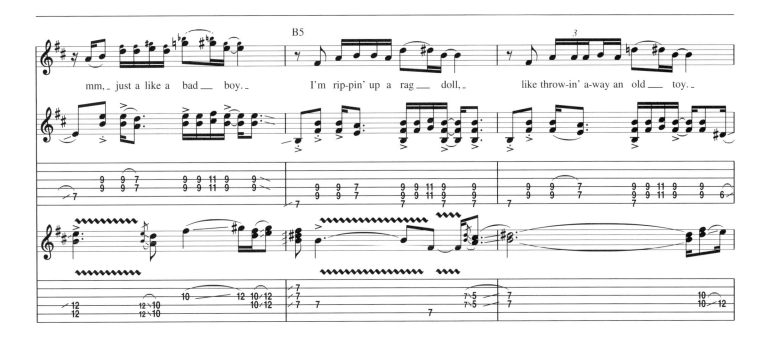

mm,_ just a like a bad__ boy.___ I'm rip-pin' up a rag__ doll,___ like throw-in' a-way an old__ toy.___

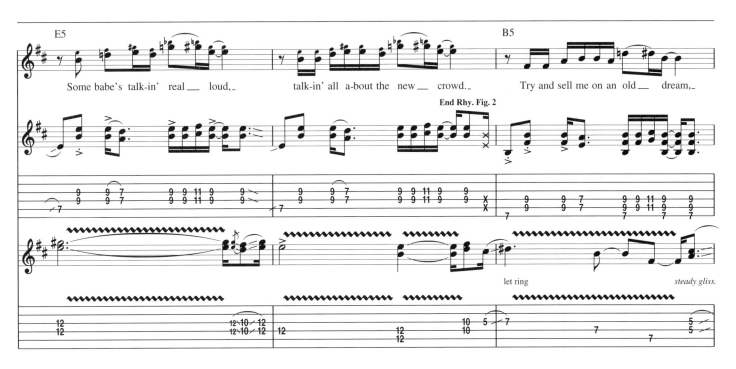

Some babe's talk-in' real__ loud,___ talk-in' all a-bout the new__ crowd.___ Try and sell me on an old__ dream,___

End Rhy. Fig. 2

let ring   steady gliss.

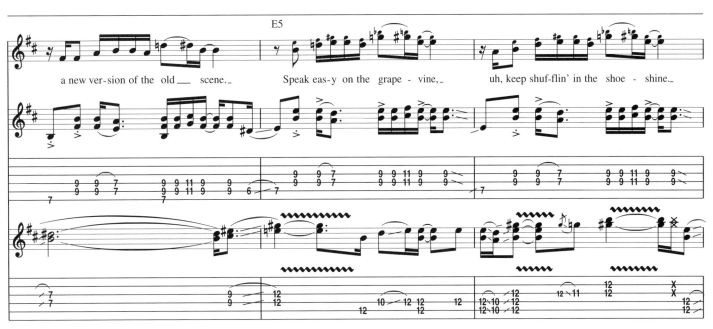

a new ver-sion of the old__ scene.___ Speak eas-y on the grape - vine,___ uh, keep shuf-flin' in the shoe - shine.___

Rag doll,   ba - by won't you do me, ba-by, won't you do me, ba-by won't you do me like you done be - fore, hoo,   hoo.

Janie's Got a Gun

Words and Music by Tyler/Hamilton

Tune Up 1/2 Step:
① = F   ④ = Eb
② = C   ⑤ = Bb
③ = Ab ⑥ = F

Intro

Moderately ♩ = 112

Dum, dum,_ dum, hon-ey what have you _ done?   Dum, dum,_ dum it's the sound of my gun.

Gtr. 1 (clean)

w/ chorus

Dum, dum,_ dum, hon-ey what have you _ done?   Dum, dum,_ dum it's the sound, it's the sound.

Nyah, nyah, nyah.   Nyah, nyah, nyah. _____

let ring - - - - - - - - - - - - - - - - - -

Nyah, nyah, nyah.   Nyah, nyah, nyah. _____

let ring - - - - - - - - - - - - - - - - - -

Chorus

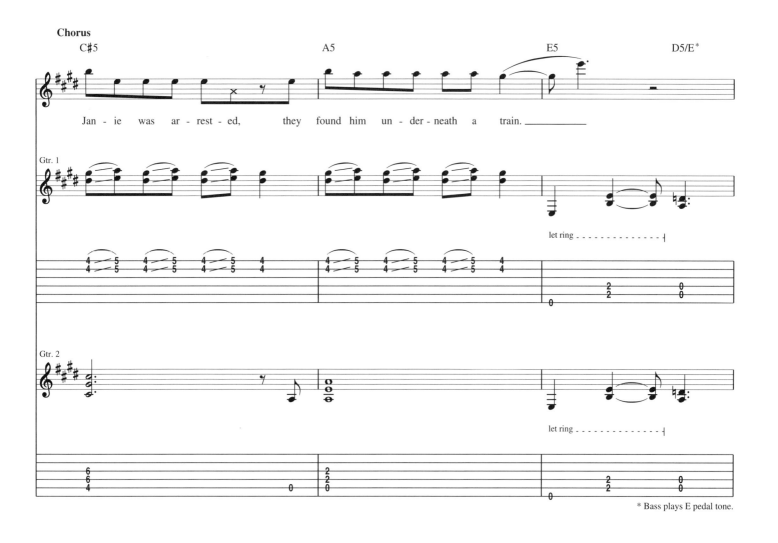

Jan-ie was ar-rest-ed, they found him un-der-neath a train. _____

Gtr. 1

let ring - - - - - - - - - - - - - -|

Gtr. 2

let ring - - - - - - - - - - - - - -|

* Bass plays E pedal tone.

But man, he had it com-in'. Now that Jan-ie's got a gun she ain't nev -

113

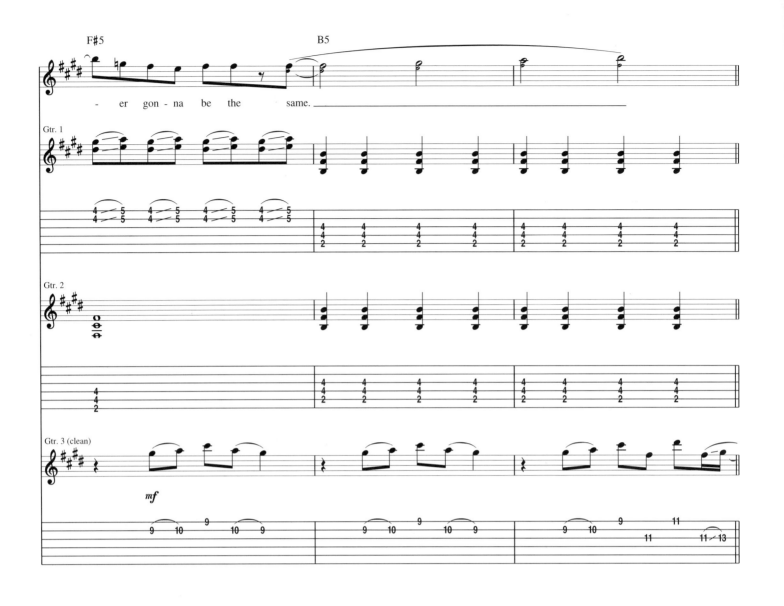

-er gon - na be the same. ____

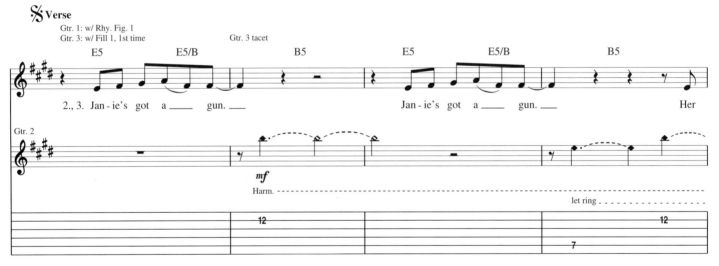

2., 3. Jan - ie's got a ____ gun. ____   Jan - ie's got a ____ gun. ____   Her

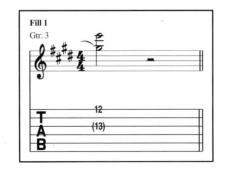

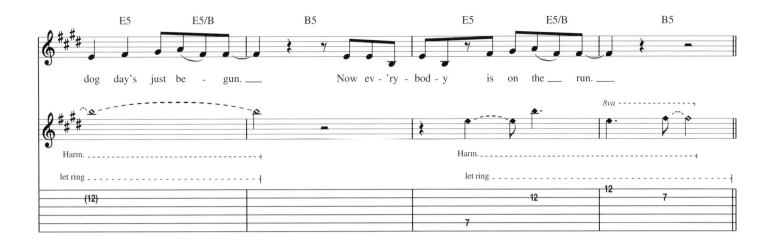

Chorus

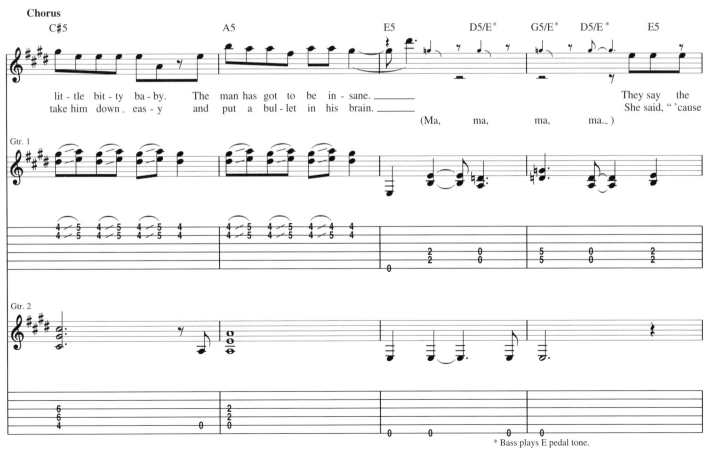

* Bass plays E pedal tone.

spell that he was un - der the light - ning and the thun - der knew that some - one had to stop the rain. __
no - bod - y be - lieves me. The man was such a sleeze. He ain't nev - er gon - na be the same."

* Bass plays E

118

Guitar Solo

D.S. al Coda

120

Love in an Elevator

Words and Music by Tyler/Perry

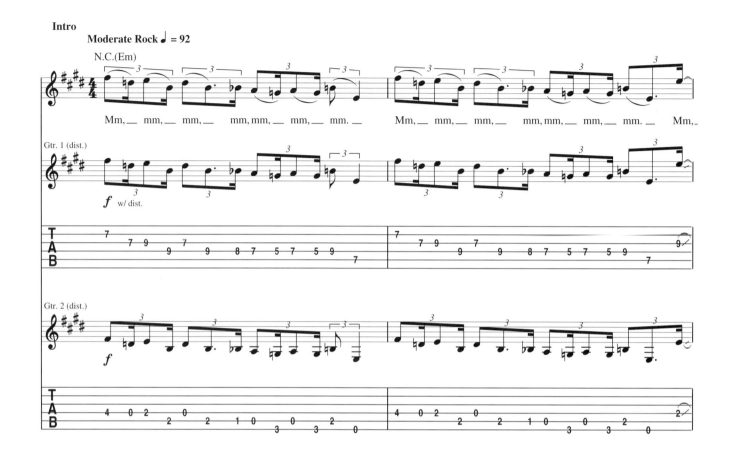

real - ly need a girl like an o - pen book __ to read be - tween the lines. _____
show you how to FAX in the mail-room room hon - ey and have ya' home _ by five." _____

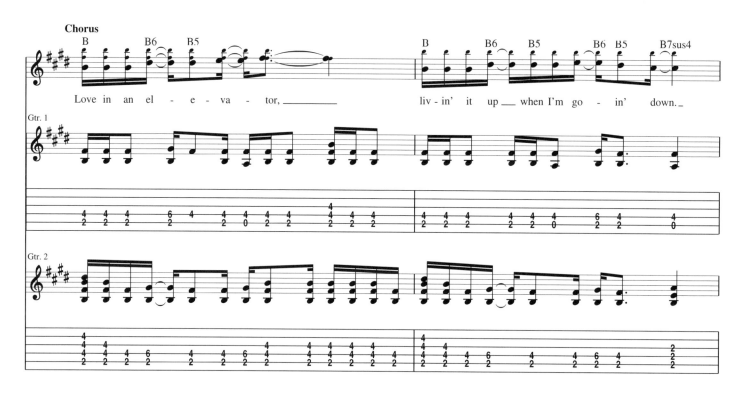

Chorus

Love in an el - e - va - tor, _____ liv - in' it up _ when I'm go - in' down. _

Gtr. 1

Gtr. 2

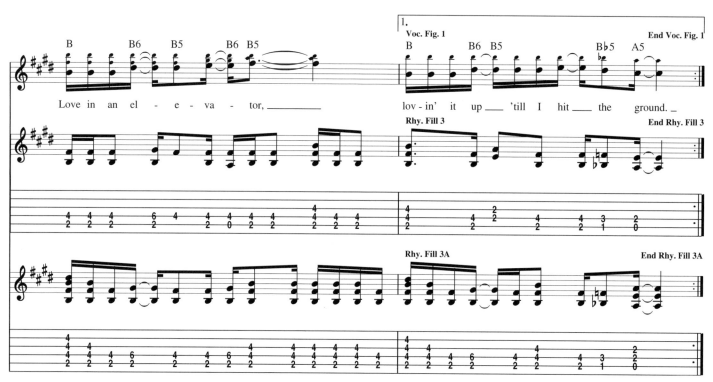

1.
Voc. Fig. 1   End Voc. Fig. 1

Love in an el - e - va - tor, _____ lov - in' it up _ 'till I hit _ the ground. _

Rhy. Fill 3   End Rhy. Fill 3

Rhy. Fill 3A   End Rhy. Fill 3A

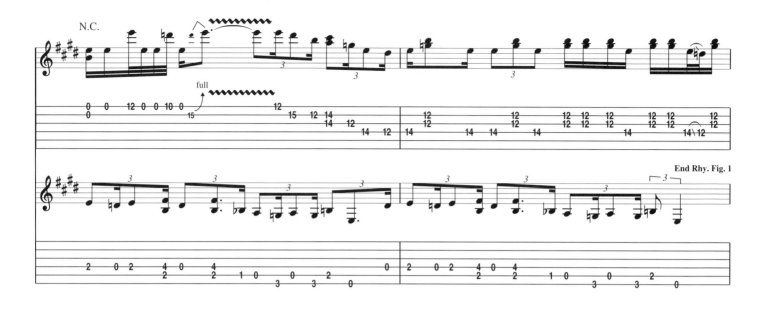

End Rhy. Fig. 1

Gtr. 2: w/ Rhy. Fig. 1, 2 1/2 times, simile

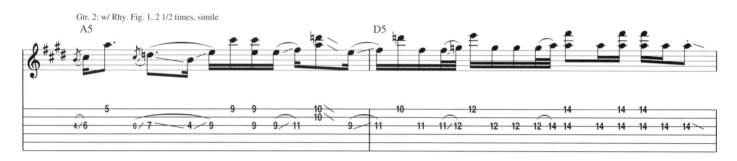

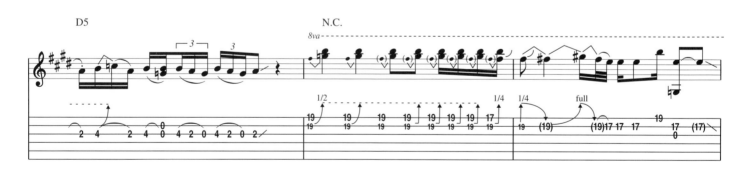

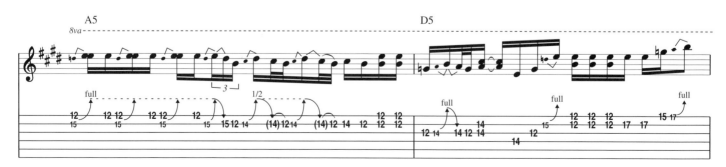

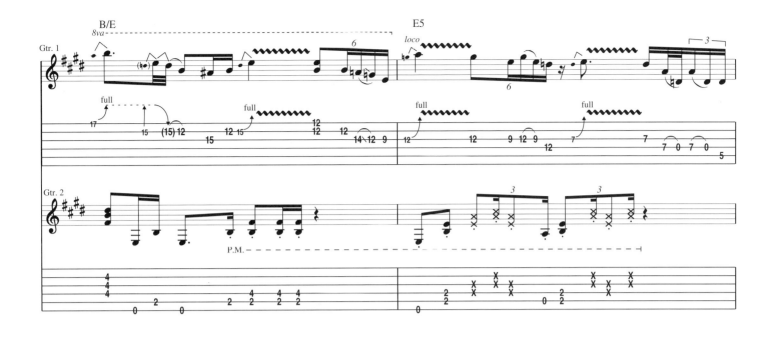

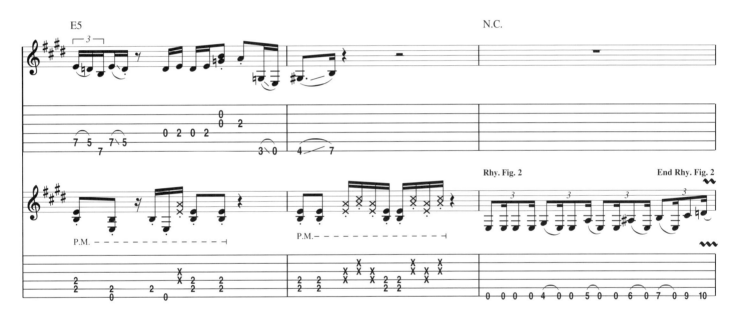

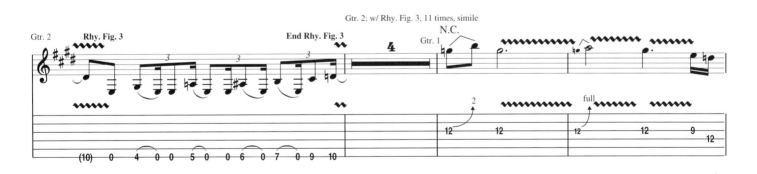

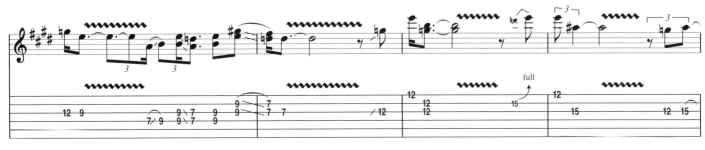

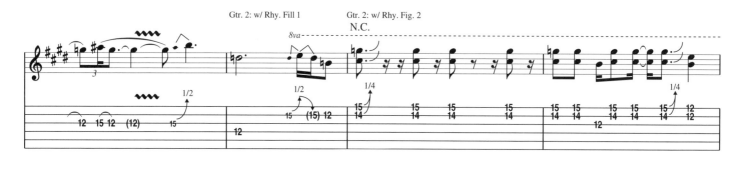

Gtr. 2: w/ Rhy. Fill 1

Gtr. 2: w/ Rhy. Fig. 2

N.C.

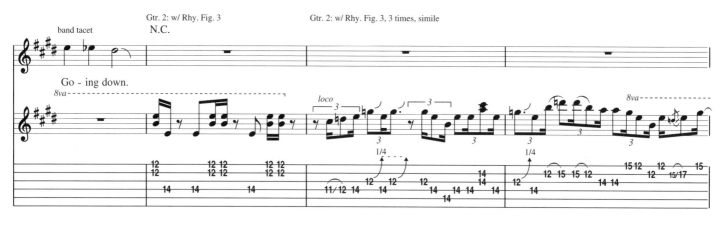

band tacet

N.C.

Go - ing down.

Gtr. 2: w/ Rhy. Fig. 3

Gtr. 2: w/ Rhy. Fig. 3, 3 times, simile

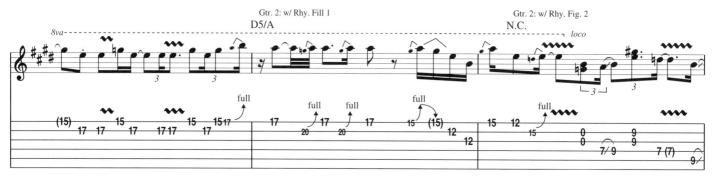

Gtr. 2: w/ Rhy. Fill 1

D5/A

Gtr. 2: w/ Rhy. Fig. 2

N.C.

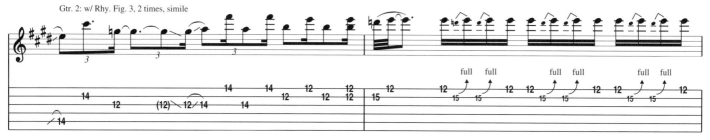

Gtr. 2: w/ Rhy. Fig. 3, 2 times, simile

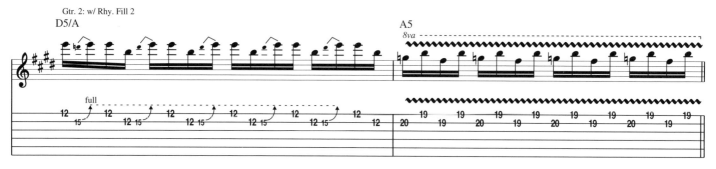

Gtr. 2: w/ Rhy. Fill 2

D5/A

A5

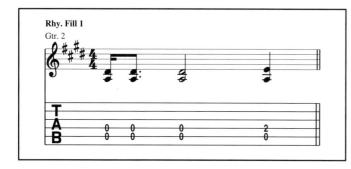

Rhy. Fill 1

Gtr. 2

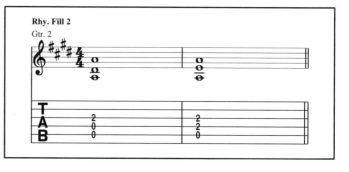

Rhy. Fill 2

Gtr. 2

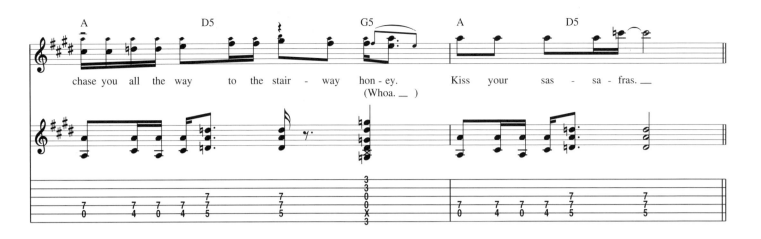

chase you all the way to the stair - way hon - ey. Kiss your sas - sa - fras. __
(Whoa. __)

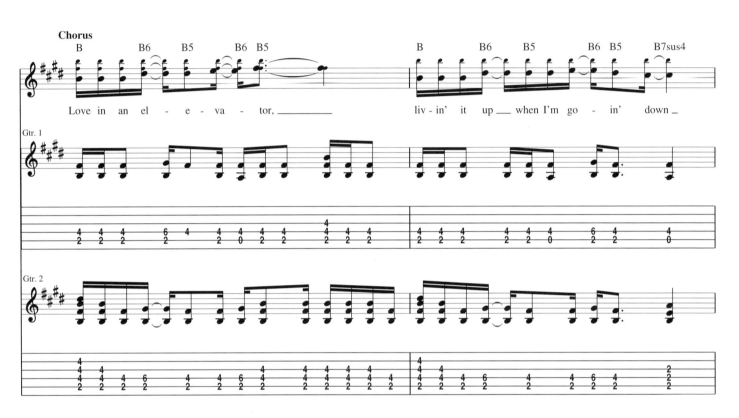

Chorus

Love in an el - e - va - tor, _____ liv - in' it up __ when I'm go - in' down __

Gtr. 1

Gtr. 2

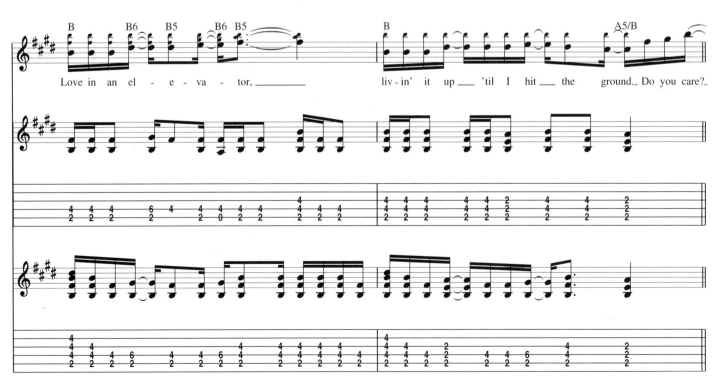

Love in an el - e - va - tor, _____ liv - in' it up __ 'til I hit __ the ground. Do you care?__

liv-in' it up ___ when I'm go - in' down. _____ Air. _____ In the air, _____ in the air, .

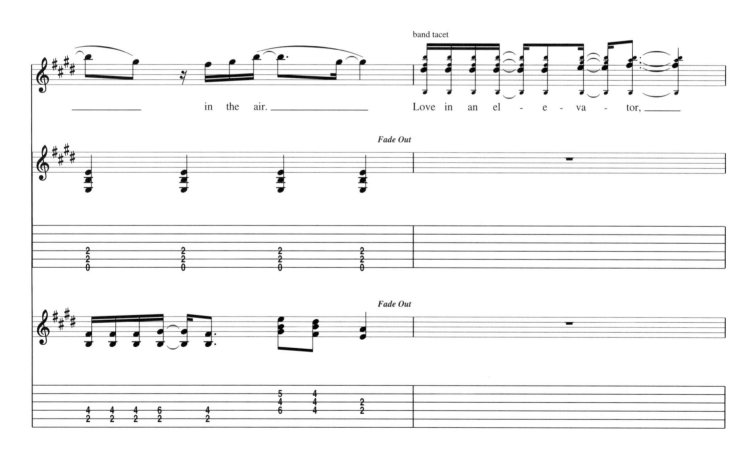

_____ in the air. _____ Love in an el - e - va - tor, _____

lov-in' it up ___ when I'm go - in' down. _____

What It Takes

Words and Music by Tyler/Perry/Child

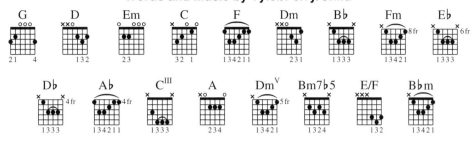

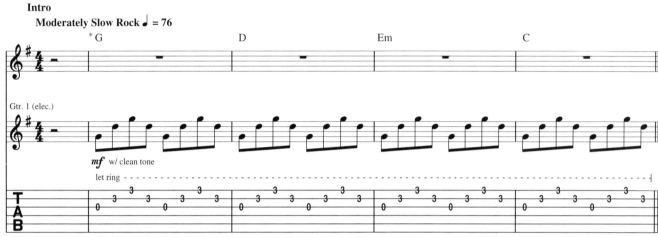

* Chord symbols reflect overall tonality.

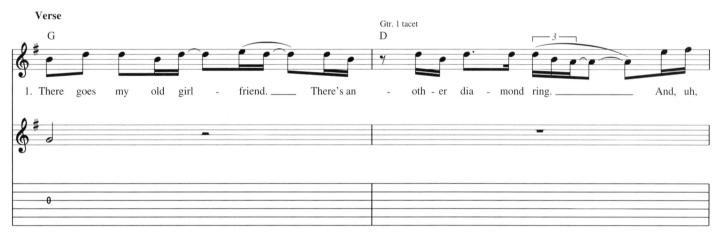

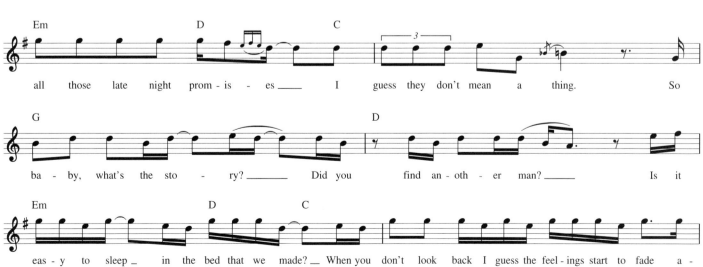

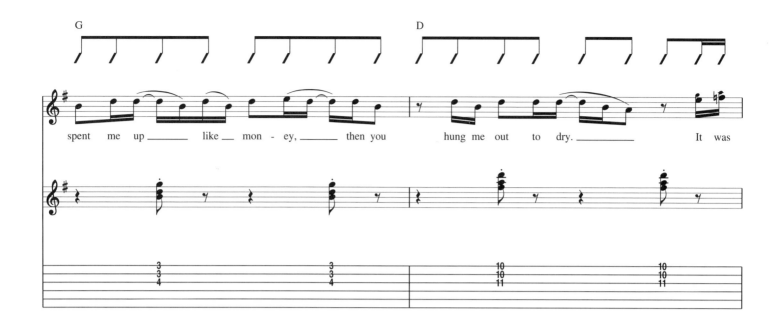

spent me up ____ like __ mon - ey, _____ then you hung me out to dry. _____ It was

D.S. al Coda

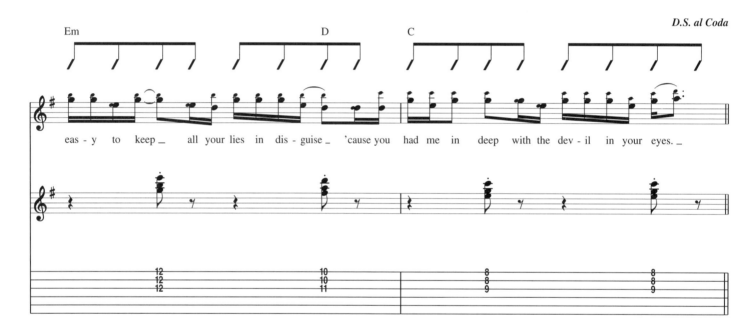

eas - y to keep __ all your lies in dis - guise _ 'cause you had me in deep with the dev - il in your eyes. _

⊕ *Coda*

Guitar Solo

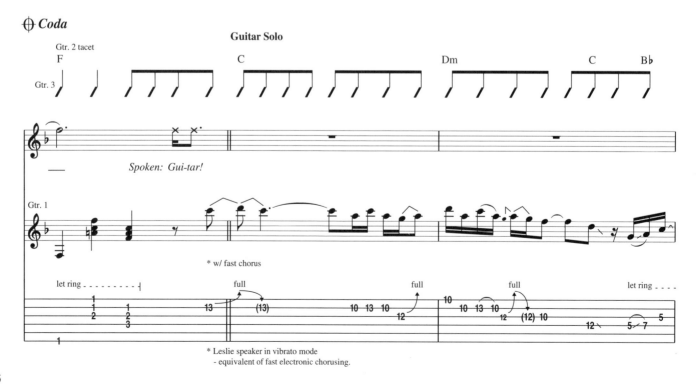

Gtr. 2 tacet

Spoken: Gui-tar!

Gtr. 1

* w/ fast chorus

* Leslie speaker in vibrato mode
  - equivalent of fast electronic chorusing.

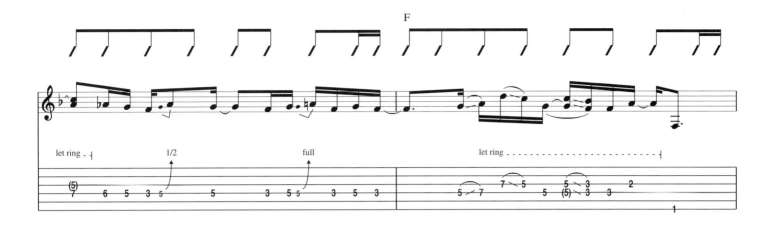

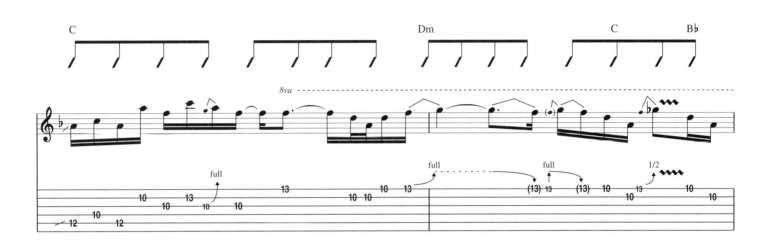

Bridge

Tell me that you're hap-py that you're on   your

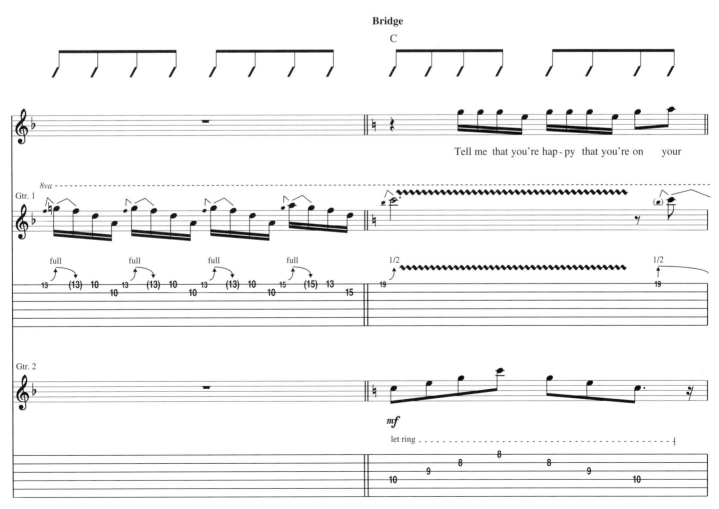

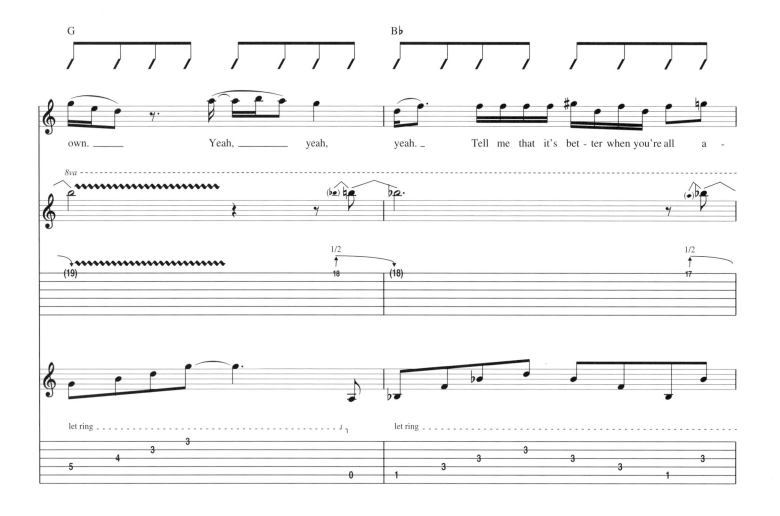

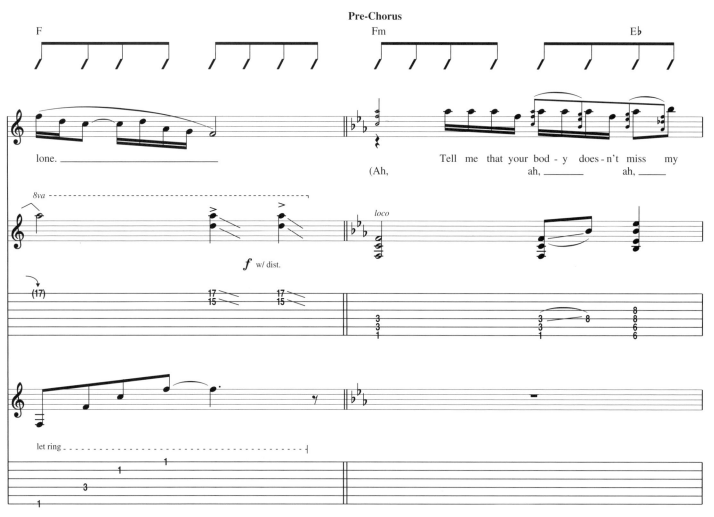

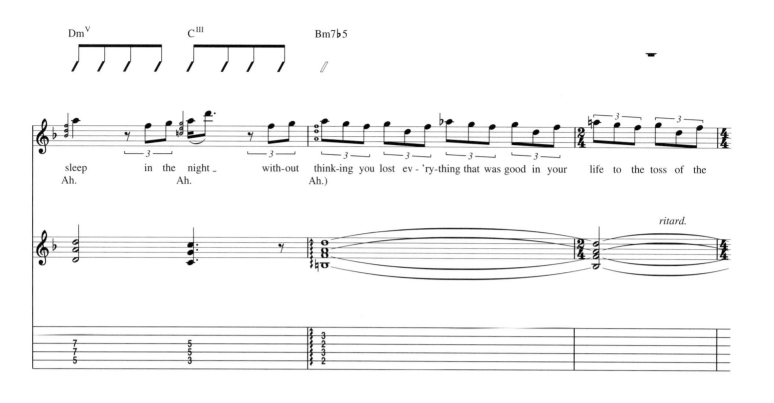

sleep | in the night | with-out | think-ing you lost ev - 'ry-thing that was good in your | life to the toss of the
Ah. | Ah. | Ah.)

ritard.

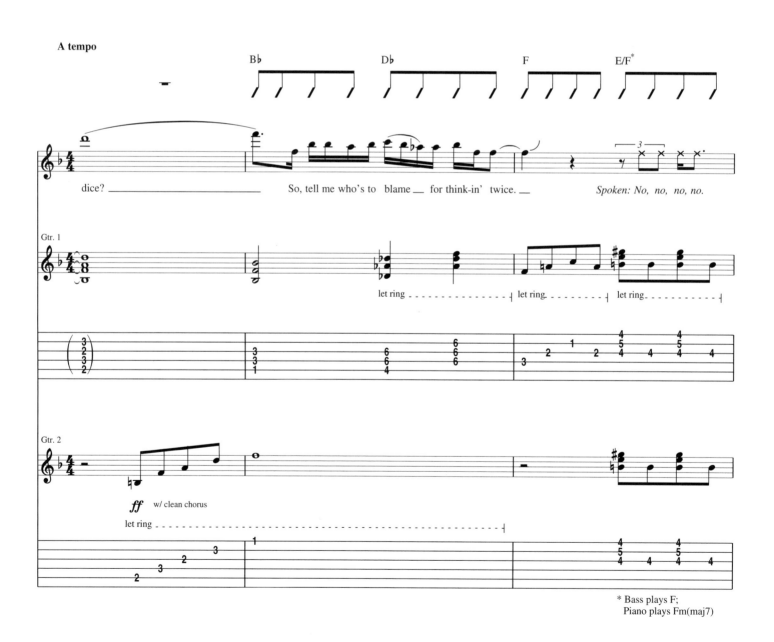

A tempo

dice? _____ So, tell me who's to blame __ for think-in' twice. __ *Spoken: No, no, no, no.*

Gtr. 1

let ring _ _ _ _ _ _ _ _ _ _ _ _ | let ring _ _ _ _ _ _ _ _ | let ring _ _ _ _ _ _ _ _ _ _ _

Gtr. 2

ff w/ clean chorus

let ring _

* Bass plays F;
Piano plays Fm(maj7)

140

'Cause I don't wan-na burn ___ in par-a-dise. ___   Ooh, _____

___   I don't, ___ I don't, ___ I don't I don't wan-na burn in par-a-dise. ___   Let it

Outro
w/ voc. ad Lib, till end
Gtr. 1: w/ Rhy. Fig. 1, 3 times

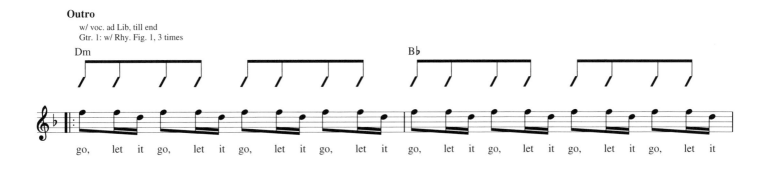

go,   let it go,   let it go,   let it go,   let it go,   let it go,   let it go,   let it go,   let it

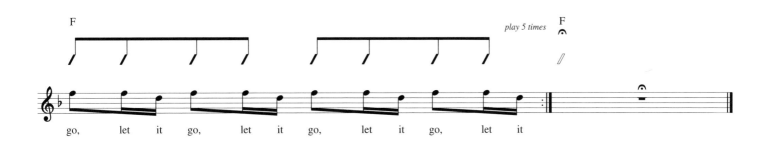

go,   let it go,   let it go,   let it go,   let it

The Other Side

Words and Music by Tyler/Vallance/Holland/Dozier/Holland

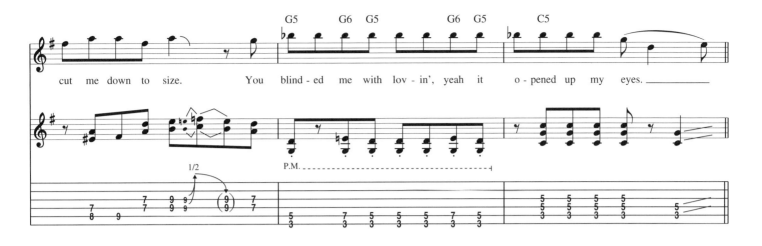

Chorus

Bkgd. Voc.: w/ Voc. Fig. 1, simile
Gtr. 1: w/ Rhy. Fig. 1

Lov - in' you has got to ___ be ___ like the dev - il and the deep blue ___ sea. ___ My

con - science's got to be my ___ guide. ___ Oh, hon - ey take me. Take, ___ take, take, ___ take, take. ___

Guitar Solo

Gtr. 1: w/ Rhy. Fig. 1, 4 times

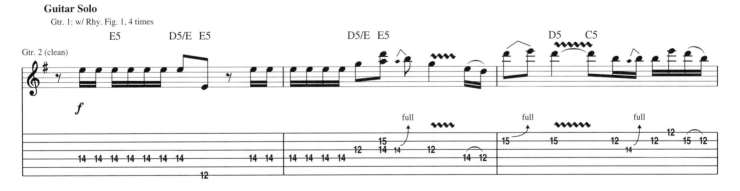

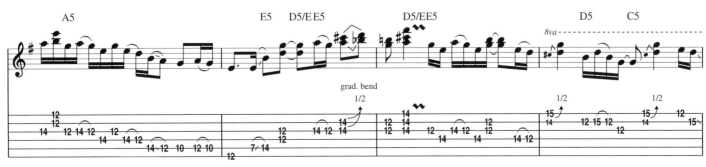

dev - il and the deep blue _ sea. _____

You know my con-science's got to be my _ guide..
For - get a - bout my fool - ish pride..

_____

Hon - ey, take _____ me to the oth - er side. _____

Outro

(w/ ad-lib lead voc., till fade)
Gtr. 1: w/ Rhy. Fig. 1, till fade

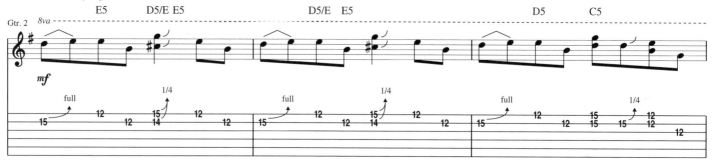

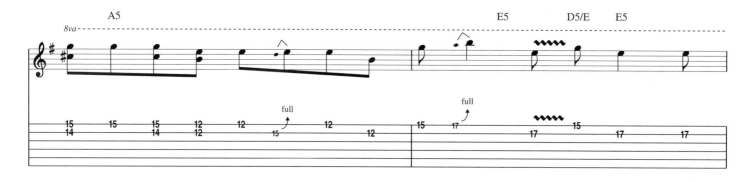

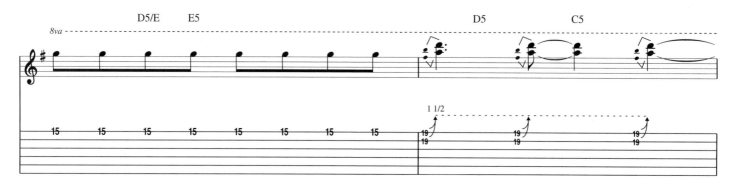

Fade Out

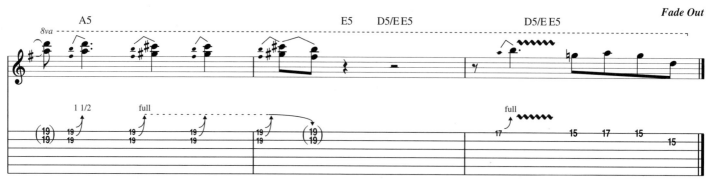

Livin' on the Edge

Words and Music by Tyler/Perry/Hudson

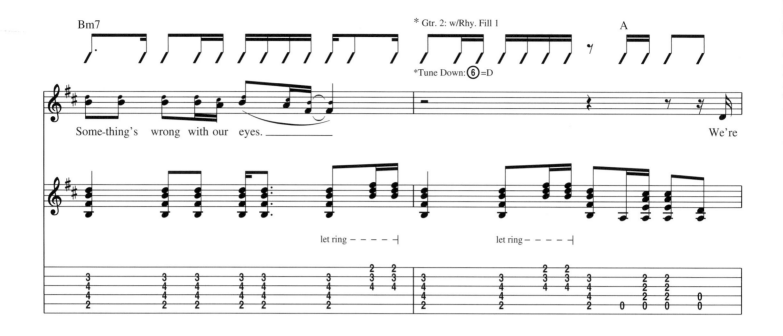

Some-thing's wrong with our eyes. _____ We're

see-ing things _____ in a diff -'rent way _____ and God knows it ain't his. _____ It

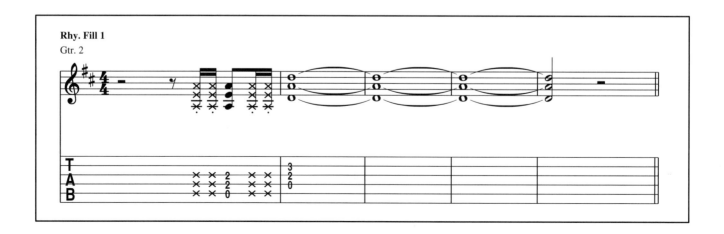

Bm7

sure ain't no sur - prise. _____ Yeah! We're liv-in' on the

let ring ____

let ring _____

*Chorus

Gtr. 3: w/Riff B, (4 times)

D5

Rhy. Fig. 1

edge.

Liv-in' on the

*Bass pedals D.

Riff A
Gtr. 1

End Riff A

f

let ring _____

sim.

full

full

Rhy. Fig. 1A
Gtr. 2

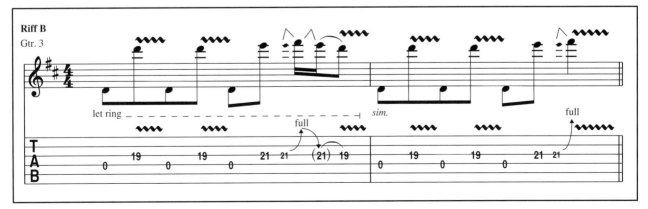

Riff B
Gtr. 3

let ring _____

sim.

full

full

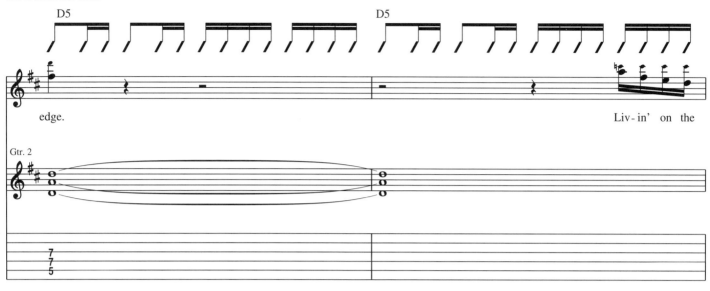

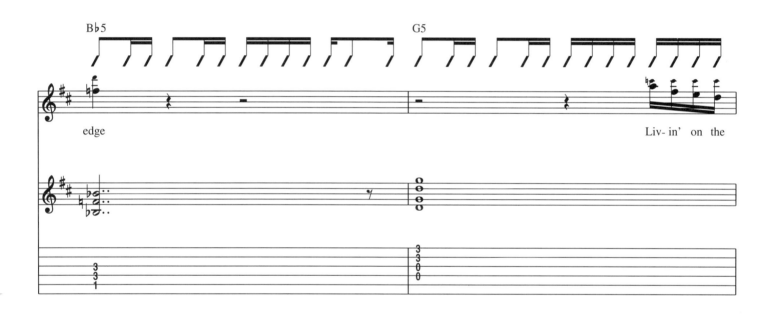

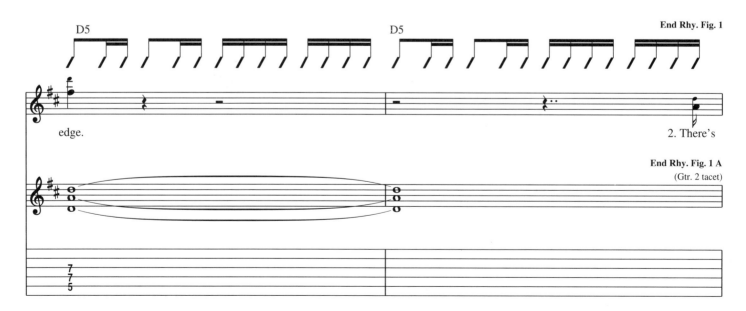

Verse

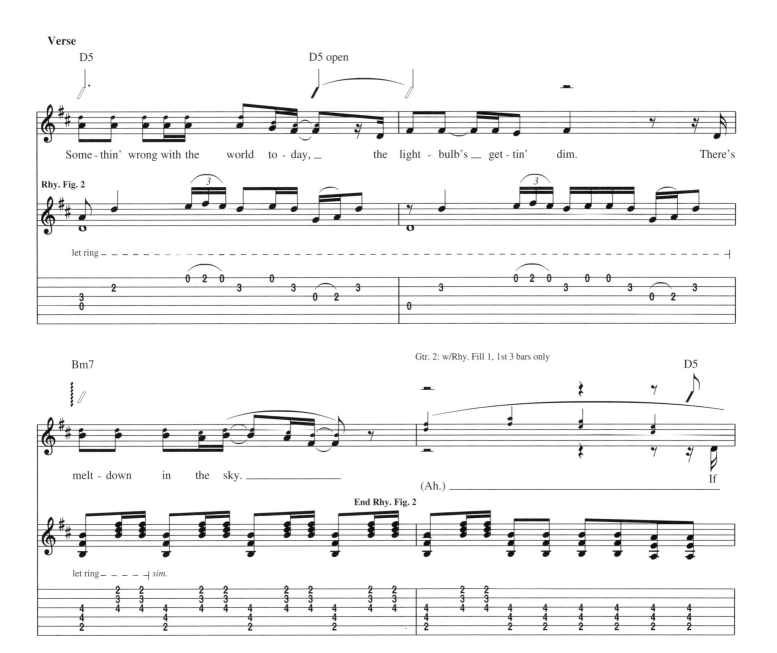

Some-thin' wrong with the world to-day, __ the light-bulb's __ get-tin' dim. There's

melt-down in the sky. __ (Ah.) __ If

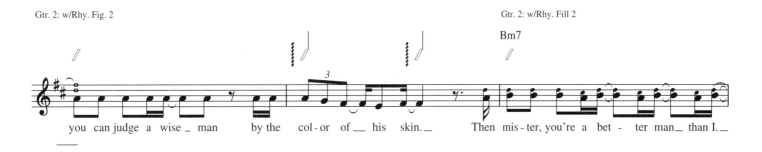

Gtr. 2: w/Rhy. Fig. 2

Gtr. 2: w/Rhy. Fill 2

you can judge a wise __ man by the col-or of __ his skin. __ Then mis-ter, you're a bet-ter man __ than I. __

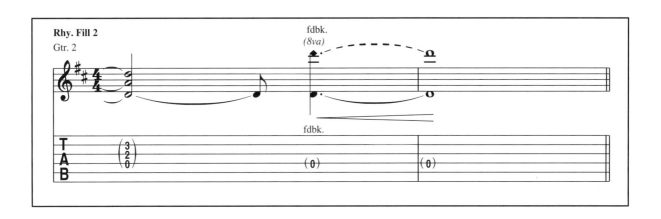

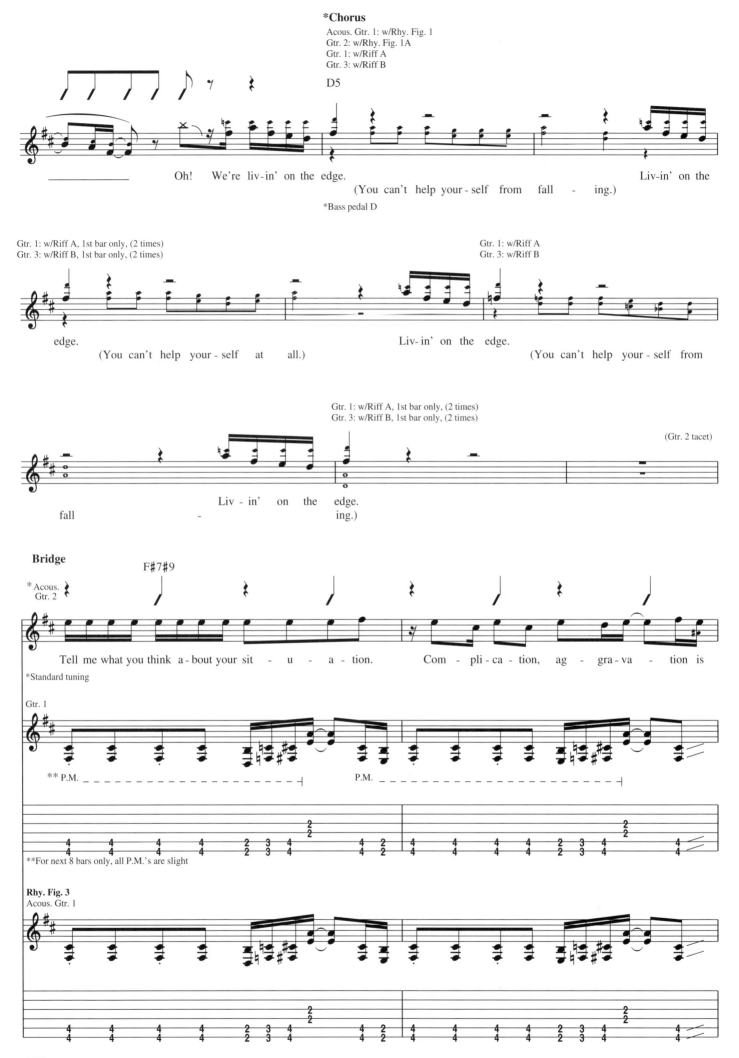

(Acous. Gtr. 2 tacet)

back___ a - gain?___ I bet you would,__ my friend, __   a -

gain and __ a - gain and __ a - gain and __ a - gain and __ a -

End Rhy. Fig. 3

Guitar Solo

Gtr. 1: w/Riff A, 1st bar only, (2 times)
Gtr. 3: w/Riff B, 1st bar only, (2 times)

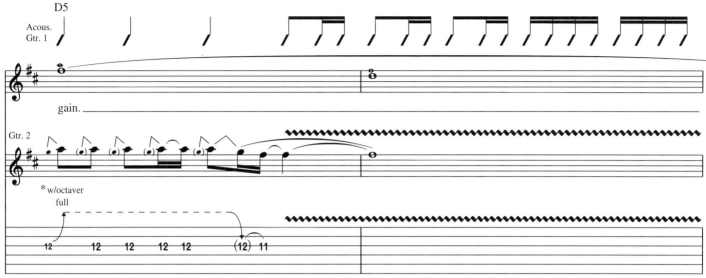

*Doubles an octave lower.

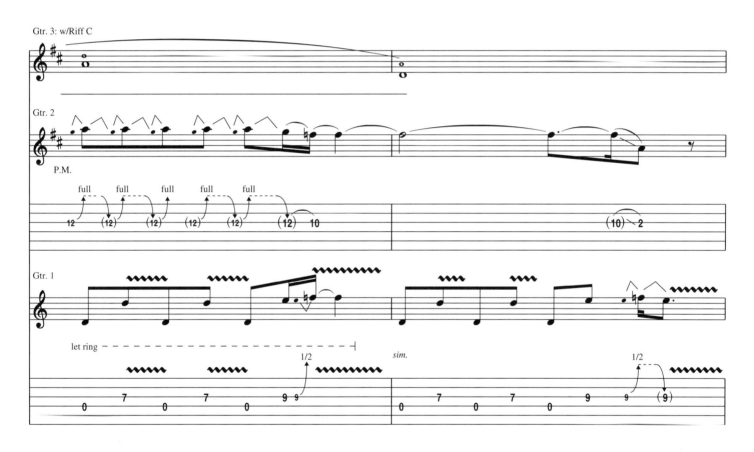

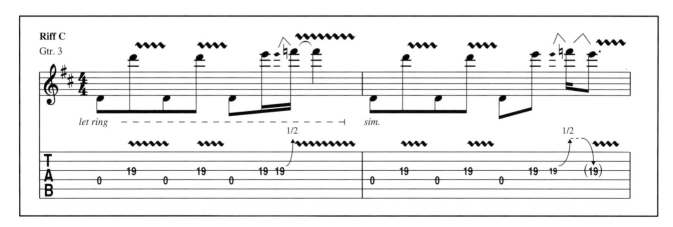

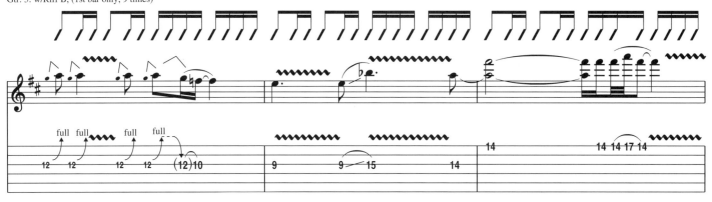

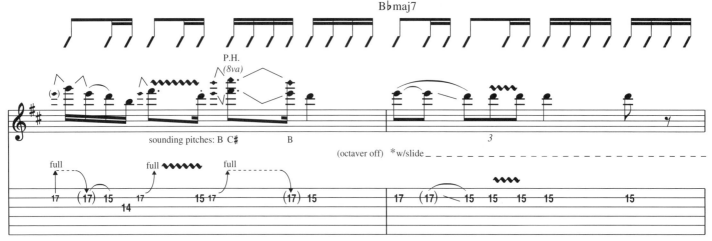

*Wear slide on pinky to allow other fret hand fingers to play single notes

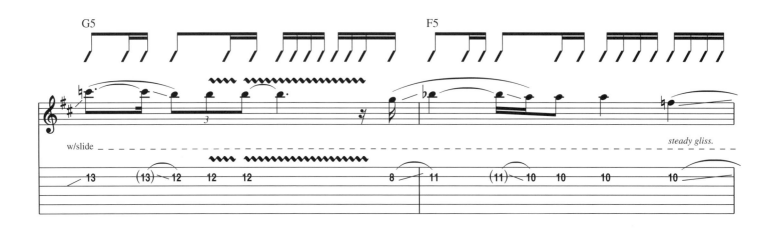

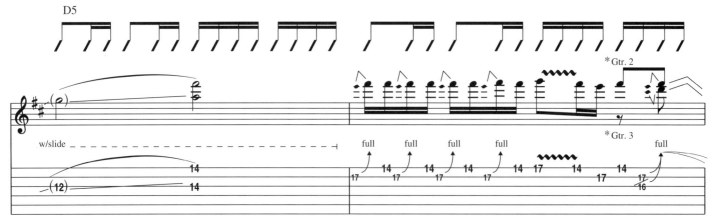

*Standard tuning

Bridge

Tell me what you think a-bout your sit - u - a - tion. Com - pli-ca - tion, ag - gra-va - tion is

get - ting to you.___ Yeah! ___ If

Chick-en Lit-tle tells you that the sky is fall - in,___ e - ven if it was would you still come crawl - ing

back _ a - gain _ I bet you would, _ my friend, _ a - gain and _ a - gain and _ a -

Verse

gain and _ a - gain. 3. There's some-thing right with the world to-day _ and ev-'ry-bod-y knows it's wrong. _ But we can

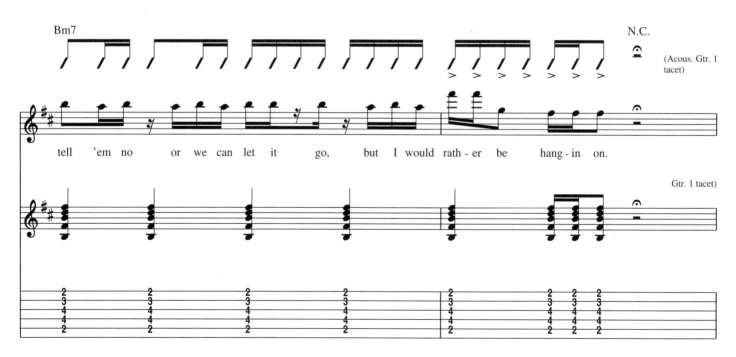

tell 'em no or we can let it go, but I would rath - er be hang - in on.

Gtr. 1: w/Riff A, (1st bar only, 9 times)
Gtr. 3: w/Riff B, (1st bar only, 9 times)
Gtr. 4: w/Riff D, till end

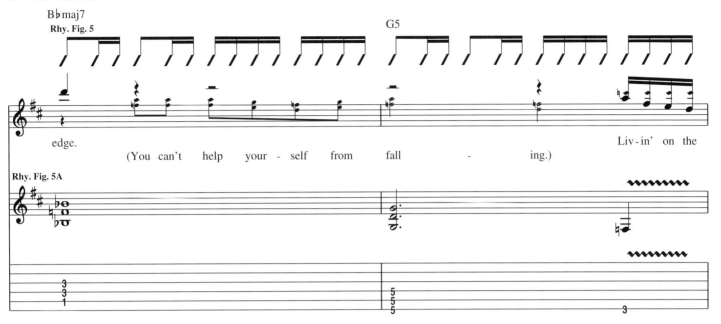

edge.

(You can't help your-self from fall - ing.)

Liv-in' on the

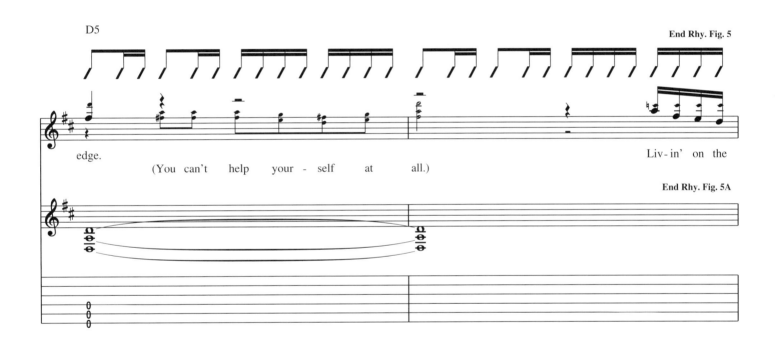

edge.

(You can't help your-self at all.)

Liv-in' on the

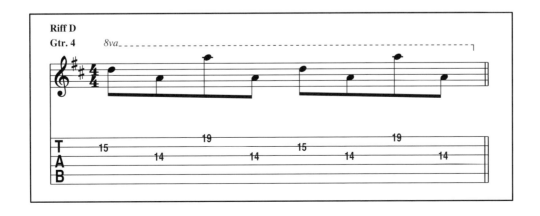

Cryin'

Words and Music by Tyler/Perry/Rhodes

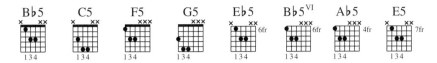

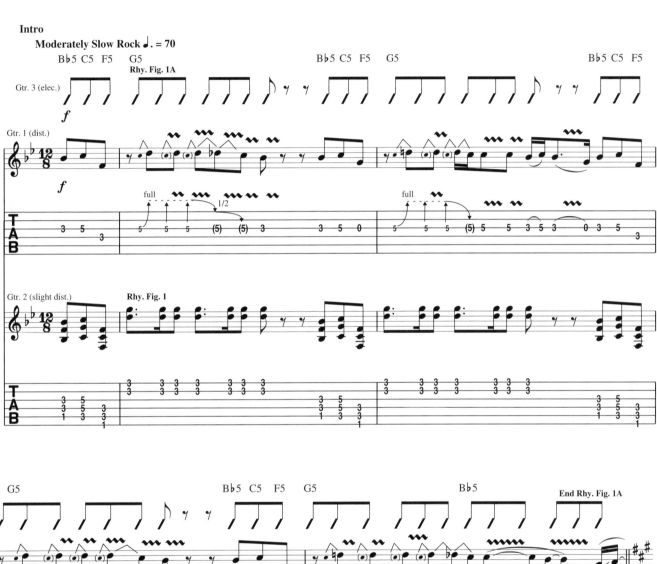

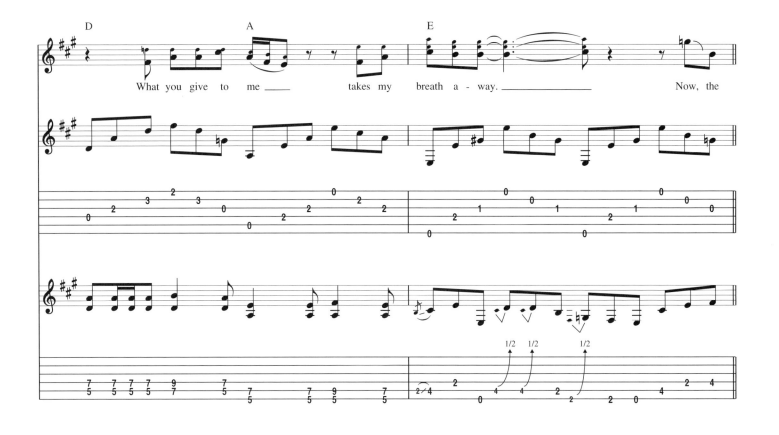

What you give to me ___ takes my breath a - way. ___ Now, the

Pre-Chorus

word out on the street ___ is the dev - il's in your kiss. If our love goes up in flames, it's a

Chorus

fire I ___ can't re - sist. ___ I was cry - in' ___ when I met you. Now I'm try - in' to for-get you.

Your love is sweet ___ mis-er-y. _____ I was cry-in' just to get you. Now I'm

dy-in' 'cause I let you ___ do what you do _____ to me. _____ Yeah!

Guitar Solo

Gtrs. 2 & 3: w/ Rhy. Figs. 1 & 1A, 1st 3 meas. only

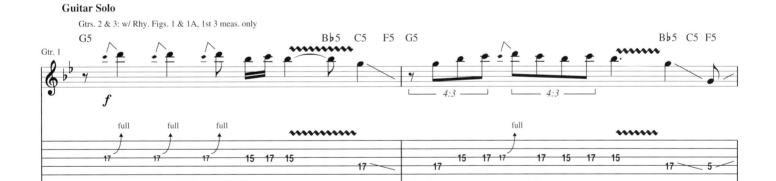

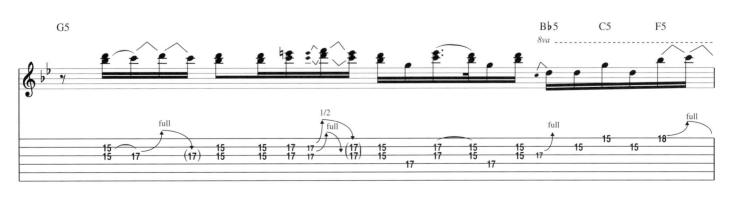

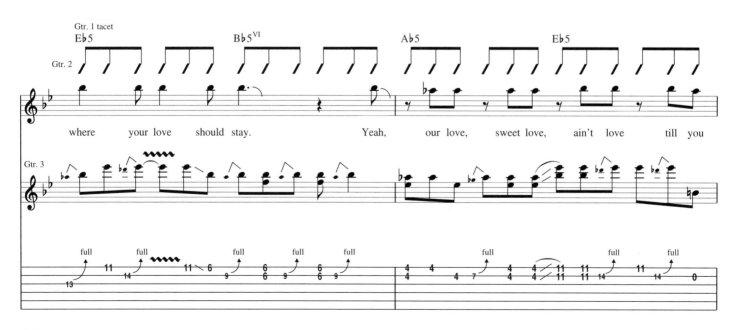

do what you, do what you do down to me, ba-by, ba-by, ba-by, ba-by, ba-by, ba-by.

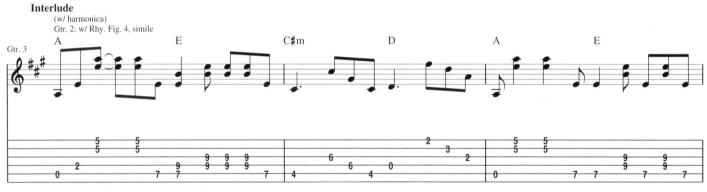

Interlude
(w/ harmonica)
Gtr. 2: w/ Rhy. Fig. 4, simile

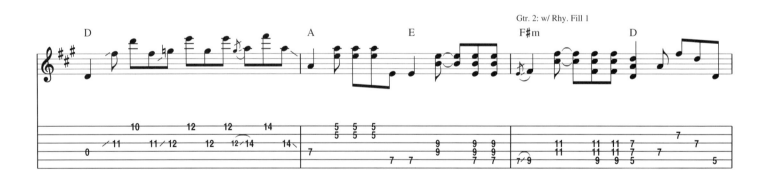

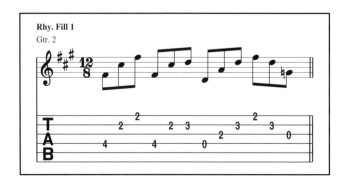

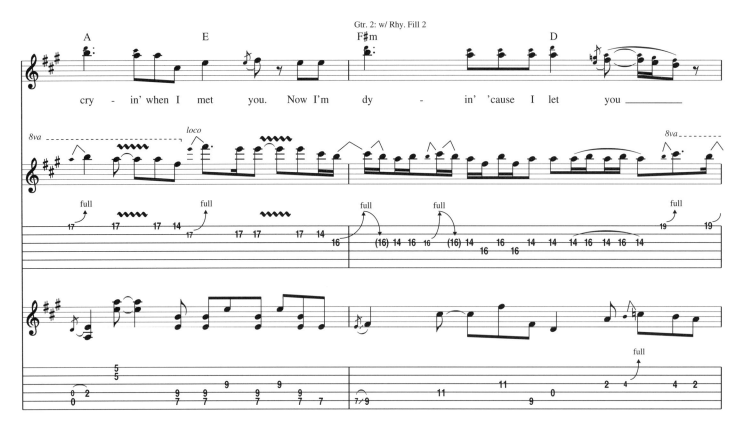

cry - in' when I met you. Now I'm dy - in' 'cause I let you _____

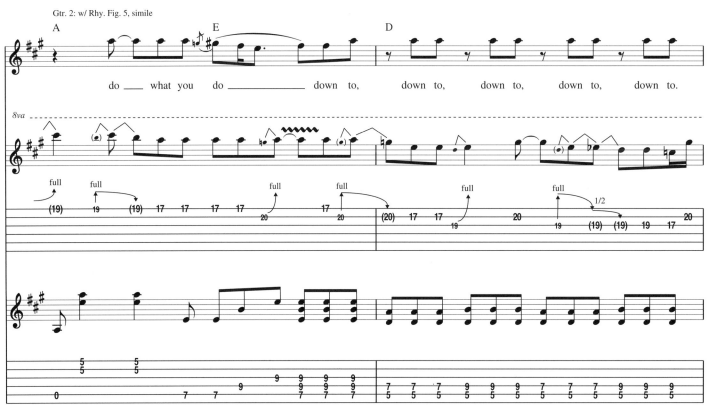

do _____ what you do _____ down to, down to, down to, down to, down to.

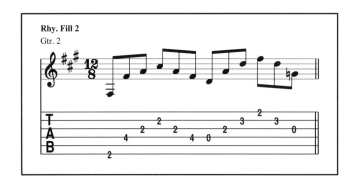

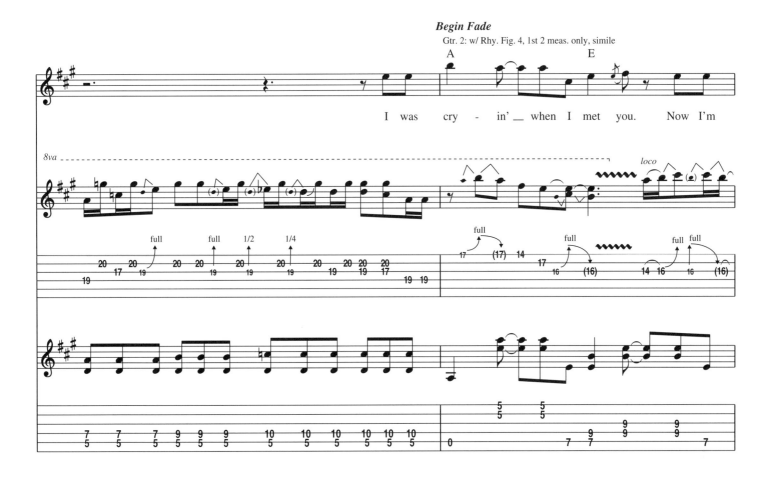

I was cry - in' __ when I met you. Now I'm

try - in' to for-get you. _____ Your __ love is sweet. _____

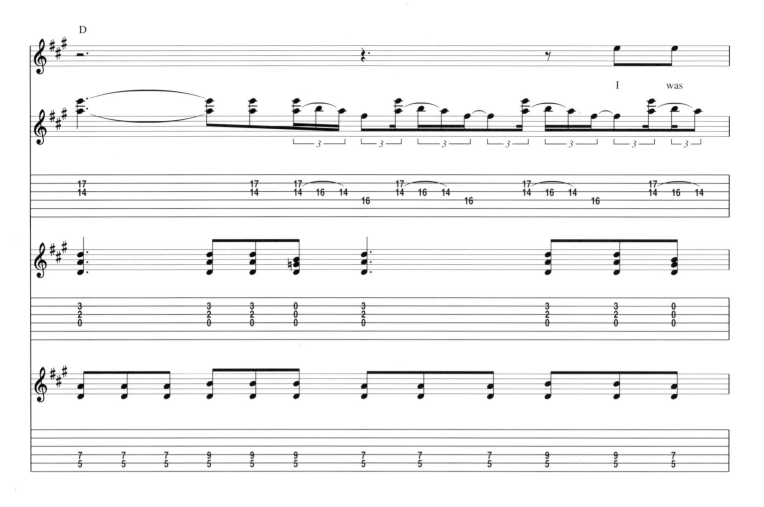

I was

Fade Out

cry - in' ___ when I met you. Now I'm dy - in' ___ 'cause I let you. ___

Amazing
(It's Amazing)

Words and Music by Tyler/Supa

*Piano arr. for gtr.
** Sampled cello arr. for gtr.

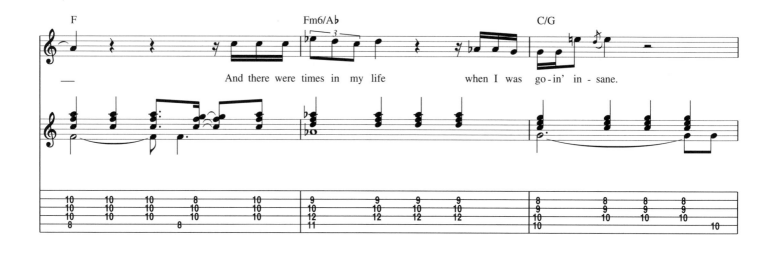

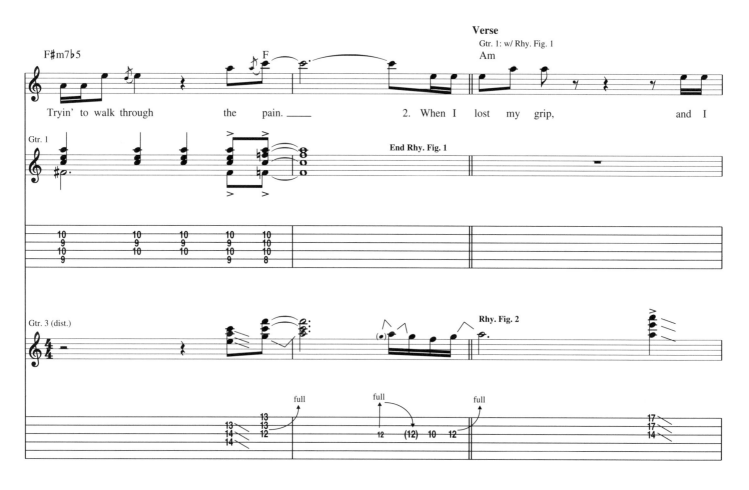

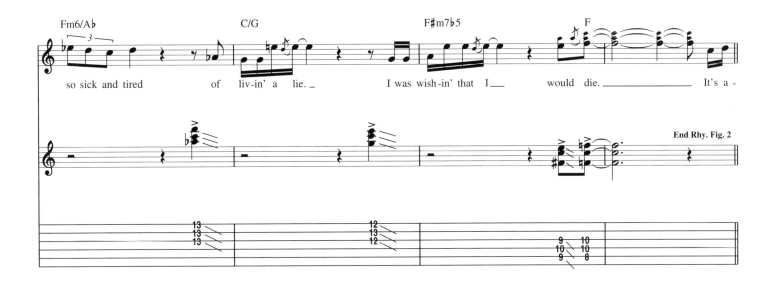

so sick and tired of liv-in' a lie. ___ I was wish-in' that I___ would die. _____ It's a -

End Rhy. Fig. 2

Fm6/A♭   C/G   F#m7♭5   F

Chorus

Gtr. 4 (dist.)

maz - ing. ___ With the blink of an eye ___ you fi - nal - ly see ___ the light, ___

let ring   let ring   let ring   let ring

C5   E5   F5   E5

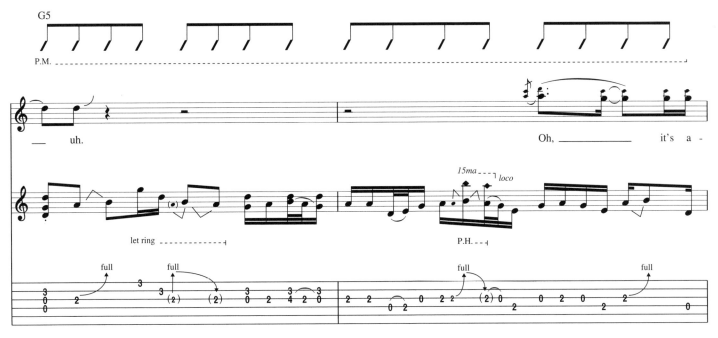

P.M.

___ uh.   Oh, _____ it's a -

let ring   P.H.   15ma   loco

full   full   full   full

G5

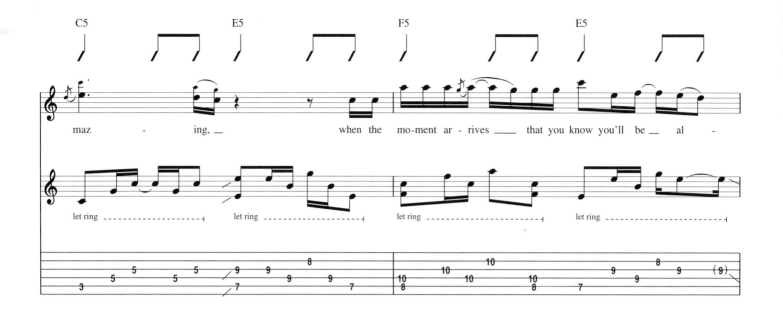

maz - ing, — when the mo-ment ar - rives ___ that you know you'll be __ al -

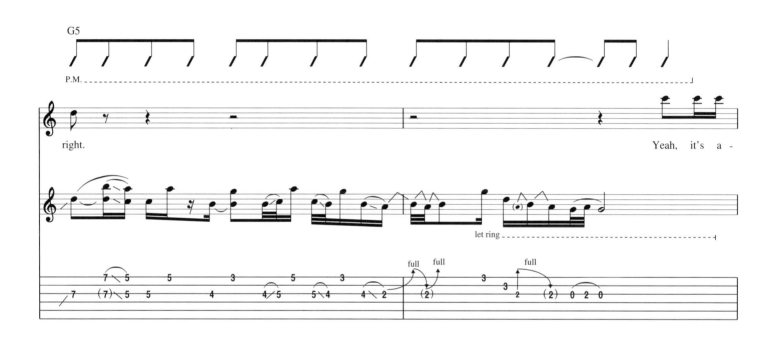

right.   Yeah, it's a -

maz - ing,   and I'm say-in' a prayer ___ for the des-per-ate hearts ___ to - night.

Verse

Gtr. 1: w/ Rhy. Fig. 1
Gtr. 3: w/ Rhy. Fig. 2

learn to crawl, __ be - fore you learn to walk. __ But I

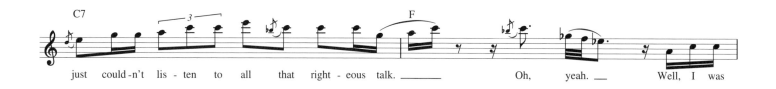

just could -n't lis - ten to all that right - eous talk. _____ Oh, yeah. __ Well, I was

w/ Bkgd. Voc. Fig. 1

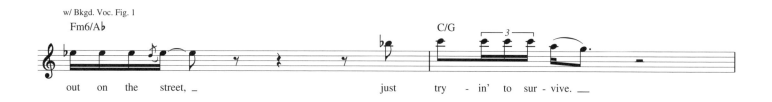

out on the street, __ just try - in' to sur - vive. __

Scratch - in' to stay __ a - live. _____ It's a -

Chorus

ma - zing, _____ with the blink of an eye __ you fi - nal - ly see - the light. __

let ring ___ let ring ___ let ring ___ let ring ___

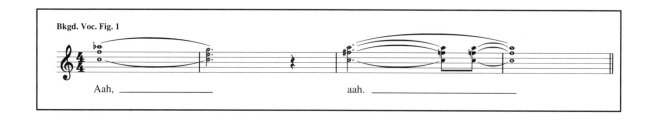

Bkgd. Voc. Fig. 1

Aah, _____ aah.

* Two gtrs. arr. for one.

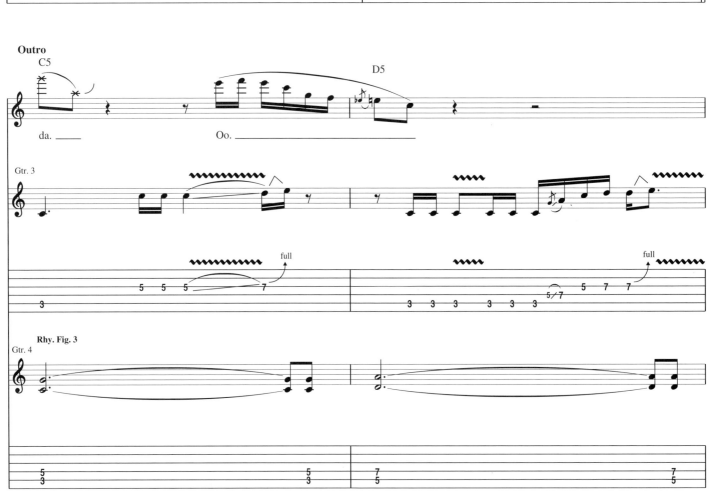

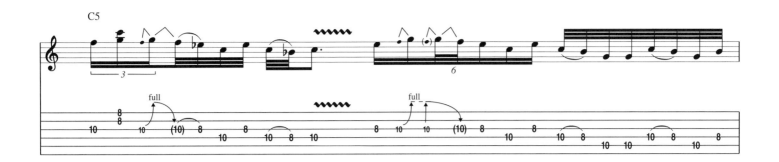

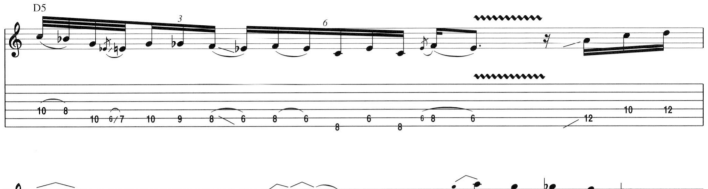

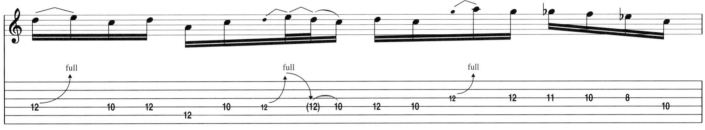

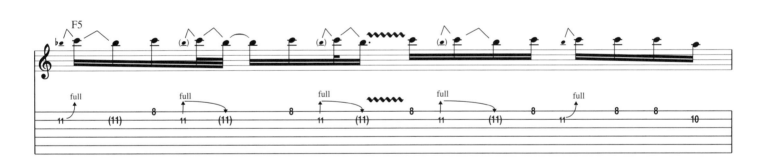

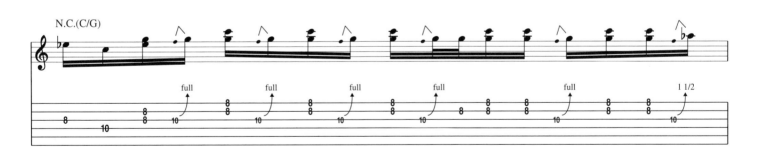

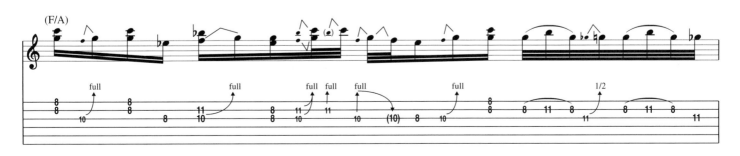

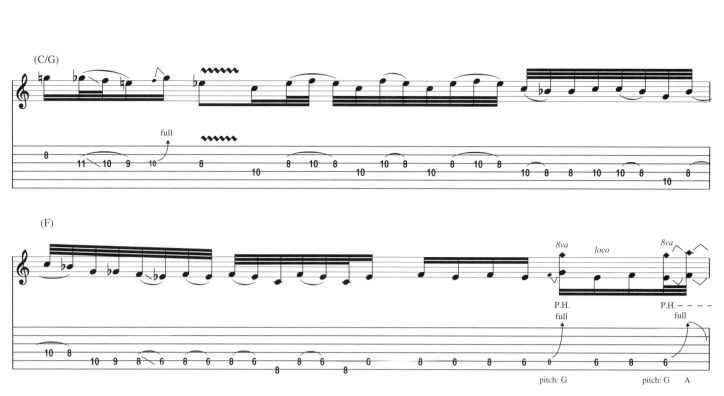

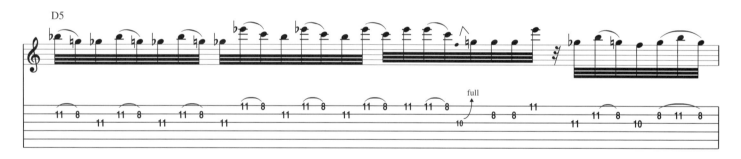

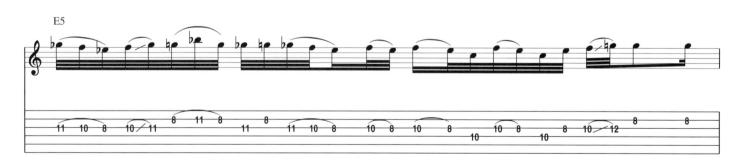

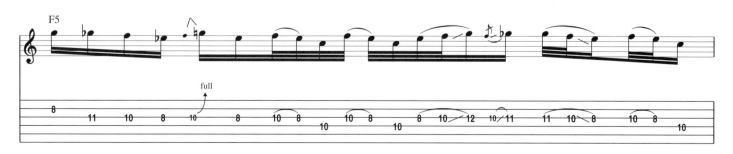

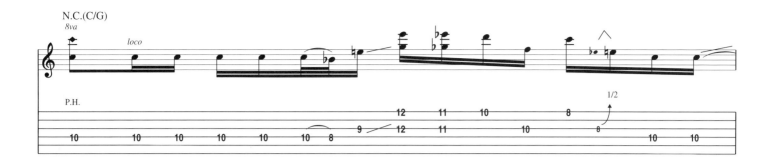

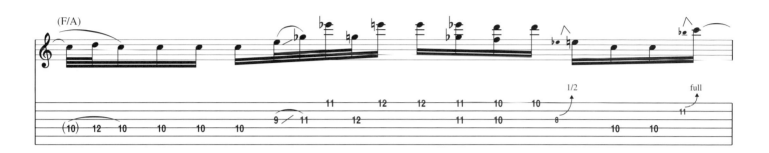

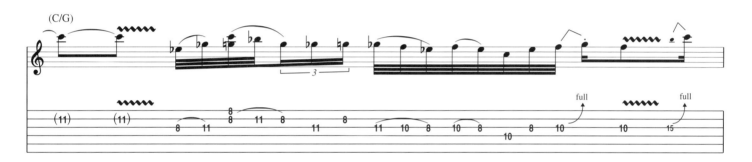

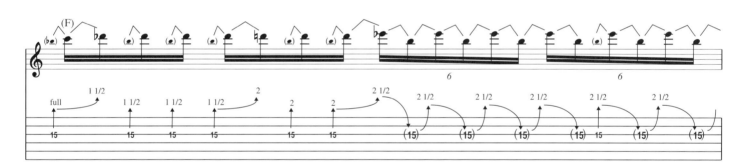

Spoken: So, from all of us in Aerosmith to all of you out there wherever you are.   Remember, the light at the end of the tunnel may be you. Good night.

Deuces Are Wild

Words and Music by Tyler/Vallance

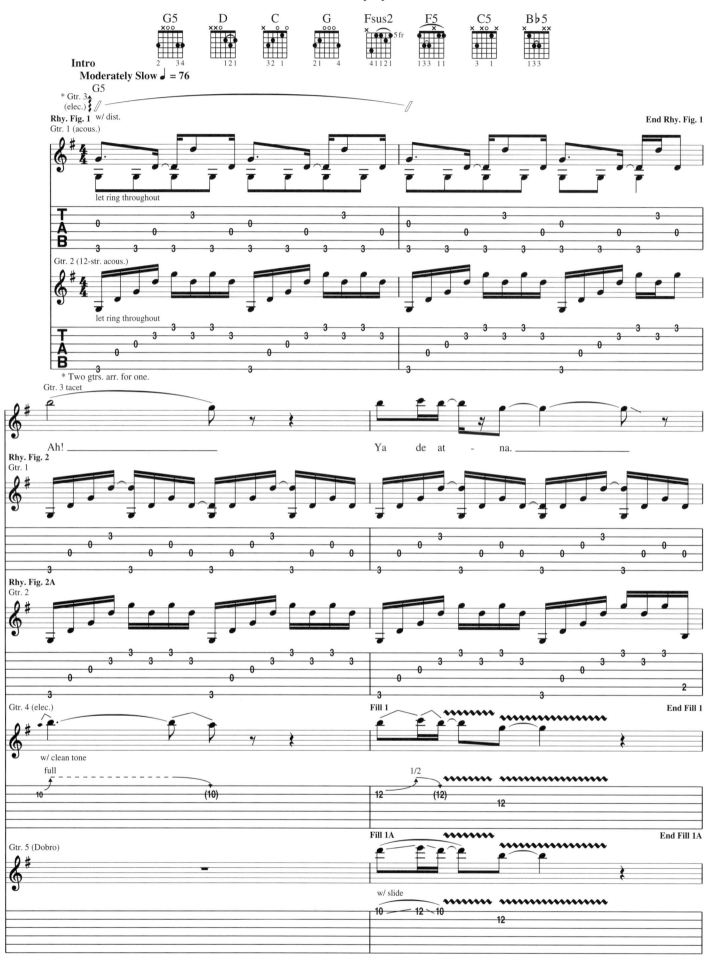

you and me is two of a kind. _____ I love you 'cause your deuc - es are wild ___ girl, like a

doub - le shot of love is so fine. _____ I been lov - ing you since you was a child, _ girl, 'cause

Gtr. 1: w/ Rhy. Fig. 1, 1/2 time

you and me is two of a kind. _____

Interlude

(w/ harmonica)

(w/ ad-lib voc.)

Wew!

w/ clean tone

* Two gtrs. arr. for one.   **Bass plays D.

* Bass plays E.

Outro Chorus
Gtrs. 3 & 5: w/ Rhy. Figs. 3 & 3A, 5 1/2 times

love you 'cause your deuc - es are wild, _ girl, { like a doub - le shot of love is so fine. _____ } I've been
yeah, a doub - le shot of love is so fine. _____
you know it, but I made up my mind. _____

1., 2.

lov - ing you since you was a child, _ girl, 'cause you and me is two of a kind. _____ I

3.

you and me is two of a kind. _____ La la di la di do.

Crazy

Words and Music by Tyler/Perry/Child

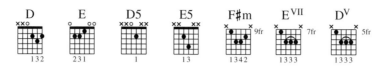

Spoken: *Come here, baby.*

You know you drive me up the wall the way you make good on all the nasty

tricks you pull. Seems like we're makin' up more than we're makin' love.

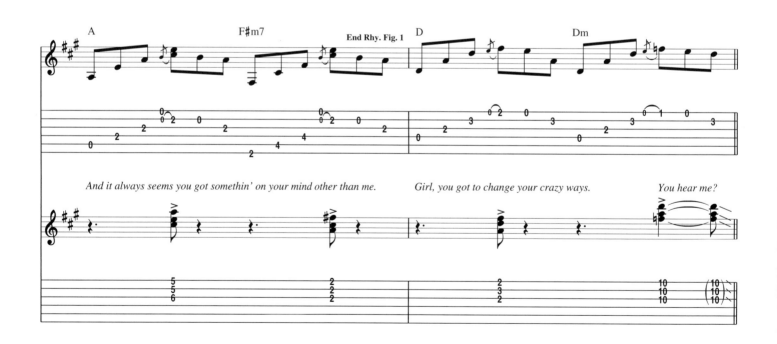

And it always seems you got somethin' on your mind other than me.

Girl, you got to change your crazy ways.

You hear me?

Verse

1. Say you're leav-in' on a sev-en thir-ty train, and that you're head-in' out to Hol - ly - wood. _

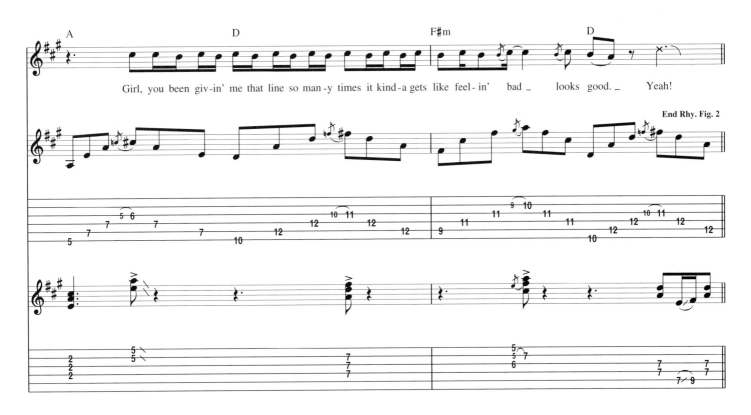

Girl, you been giv-in' me that line so man-y times it kind-a gets like feel-in' bad _ looks good. _ Yeah!

Fill 1
*Gtr. 3 (slight dist.)

* Two Gtrs. arr. for one.

Chorus

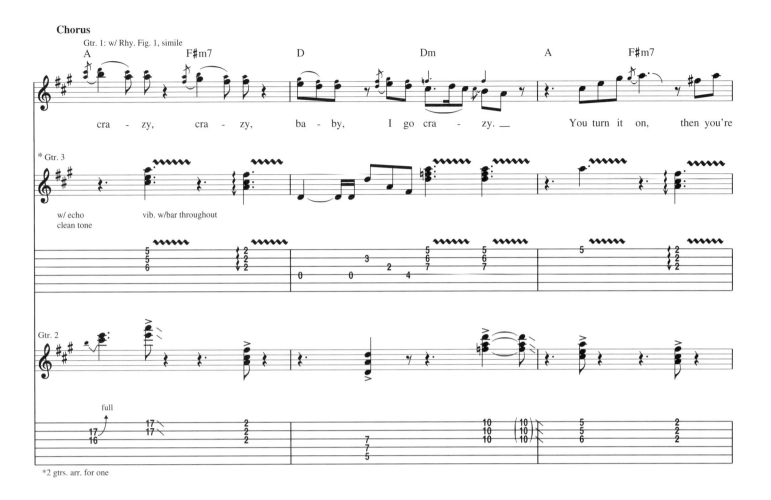

cra - zy, cra - zy, ba - by, I go cra - zy. ___ You turn it on, then you're

gone. ___ Yeah, you drive ___ me cra - zy, cra - zy, cra - zy for you ba - by. ___

Gtr. 1: w/ Rhy. Fill 1

What can I do, ___ hon - ey? I feel like the col - or ___ blue. ___

Verse
Gtr. 3 tacet
Gtr. 1: w/ Rhy. Fig. 2, simile

2. You're pack-in' up your _ stuff, and talk-in' like it's tough and try-in' to tell me that it's time to go. ___ Yeah!

*Gtr. 4

Gtr. 2

*Mandolin arr. for gtr.

Rhy. Fill 1
Gtr. 1

But, I know you ain't wear-in' noth-in' un-der-neath that o-ver-coat. ___ And it's all a show. _ Yeah!

Pre-Chorus

That kind - a lov-in' makes me wan-na pull ___ down the shade. _ Yeah!

Fill 3
Gtr. 3

That _ kind-a lov-in', yeah, now I'm nev-er, nev-er, nev-er, _ nev-er gon-na be the same. I go

Chorus

Gtr. 4 tacet
Gtr. 1: w/ Rhy. Fig. 1, simile

cra - zy, cra - zy, ba - by, I go cra - zy. _ You turn it on, then you're

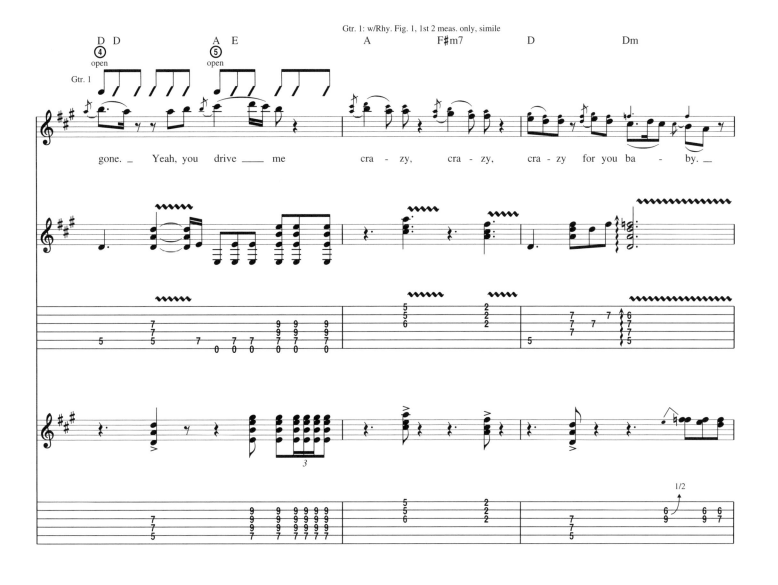

gone. _ Yeah, you drive ____ me cra-zy, cra-zy, cra-zy for you ba - by. _

What can I do, ____ hon - ey? I feel like the col - or ____ blue. _____

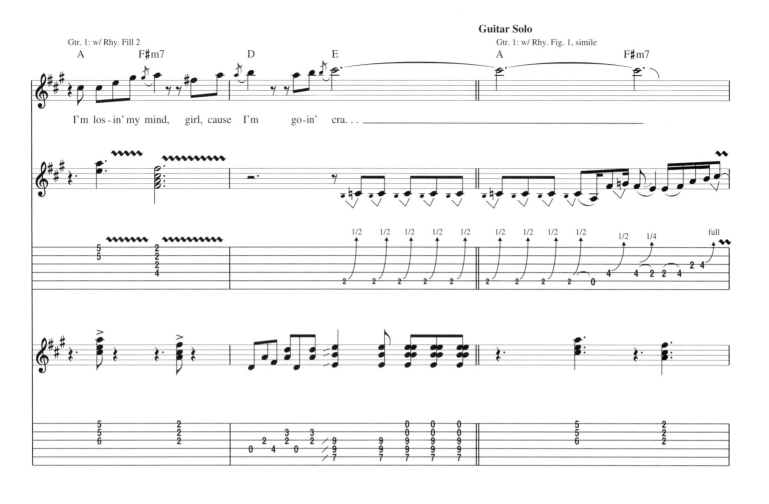

I'm los-in' my mind, girl, cause I'm go-in' cra. . .

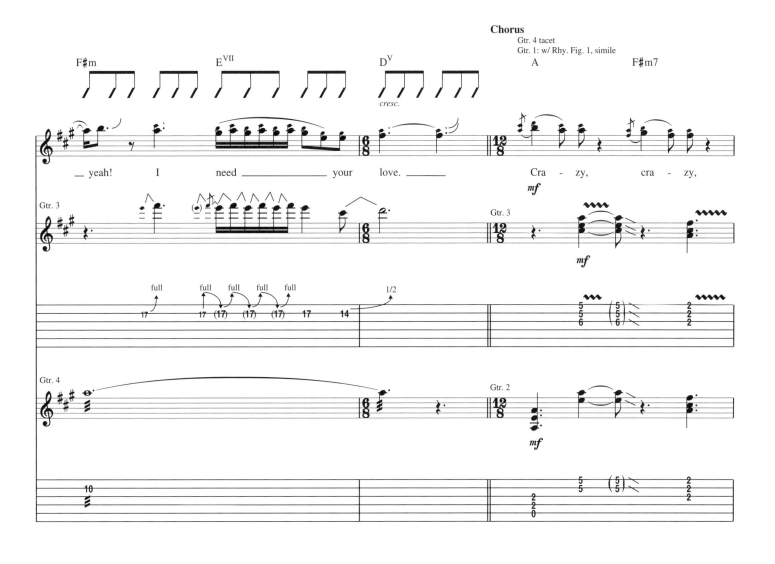

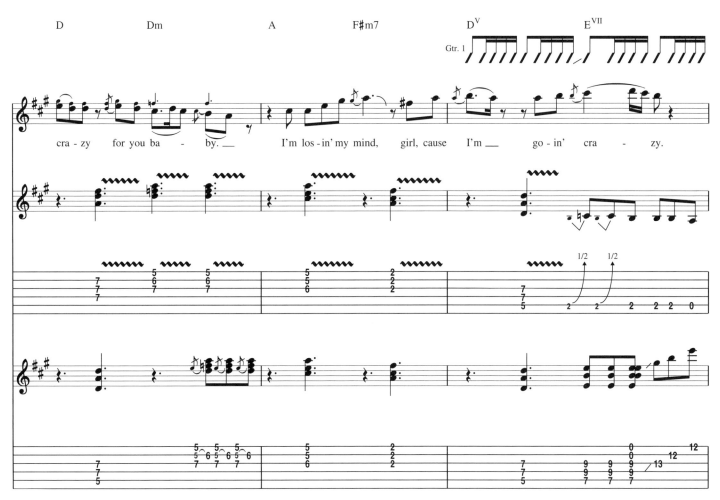

Outro

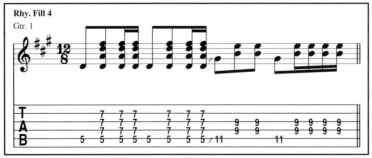

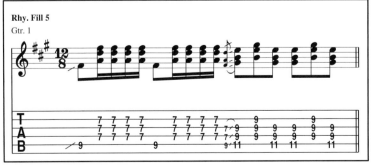

Falling in Love (Is Hard on the Knees)

Words and Music by Tyler/Perry/Ballard

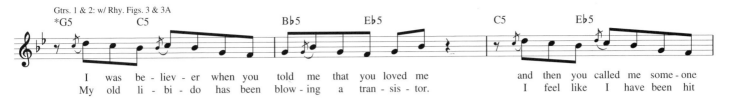

Gtrs. 1 & 2: w/ Rhy. Figs. 3 & 3A

*G5   C5   Bb5   Eb5   C5   Eb5

I was be-liev-er when you told me that you loved me   and then you called me some-one
My old li-bi-do has been blow-ing a tran-sis-tor.   I feel like I have been hit

* Chord symbols reflect combined tonality.

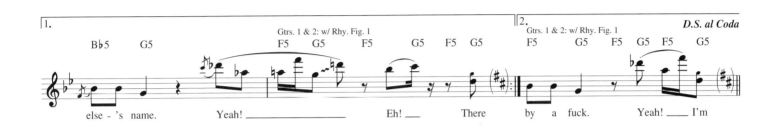

1.
Bb5 G5   F5 G5 F5 G5 F5 G5

2. Gtrs. 1 & 2: w/ Rhy. Fig. 1   *D.S. al Coda*
F5   G5 F5 G5 F5 G5

else-'s name.   Yeah! _____   Eh! ___   There   by a fuck.   Yeah! ___ I'm

⊕ *Coda*   **Bridge**
F5 G5   F#5 G#5   G5 A5   G#5 A#5   A5 B5   Bb5   C5

Gtr. 2
P.M.

What are you look-ing for?

Gtrs. 1 & 2   Gtr. 1

1/2

```
8        10        10
8        10        10
3  5  5  4  6  6  5  7   7  6  8    8  7  9  9  8      10  10      10
3  5  5  4  6  6  5  7   7  6  8    8  7  9  9  8
1  3  3  2    4  4  3  5   5  4  6    6  5    7  6
```

Bb5 C5
P.M.

It's got to be hard-core.   Must be some kind of nov-veau riche. _____

1/2   1/2   1/2

```
8        10        10      8        10        10      8        10        10
8        10        10      8        10        10      8        10        10
10  10      10            10  10      10            10  10      10
```

Is this your on - ly chance   or some hyp - not - ic trance?   Let's get you on a tight - er

Guitar Solo

Gtr. 2: w/ Rhy. Fig. 2

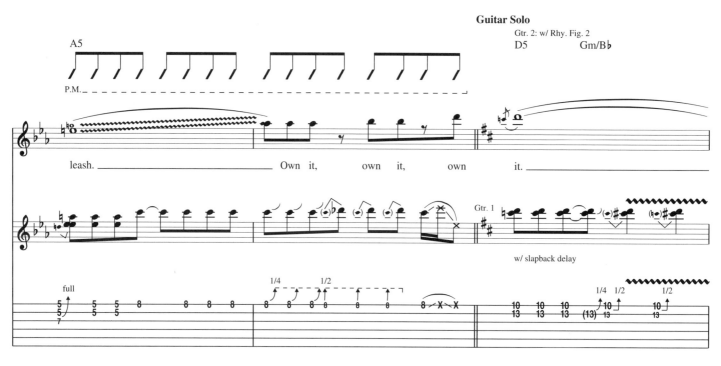

leash. _____   Own it,   own it,   own   it. _____

w/ slapback delay

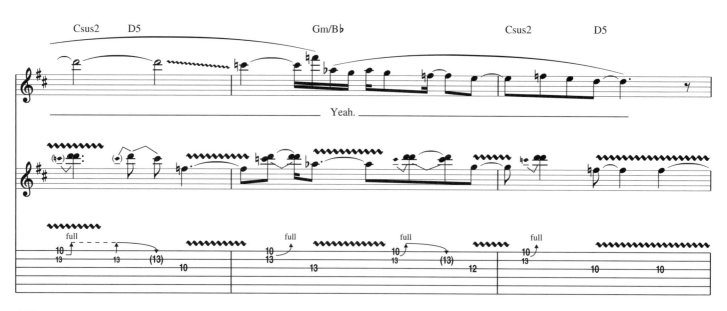

Yeah.

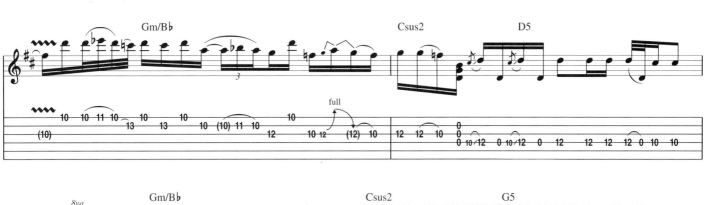

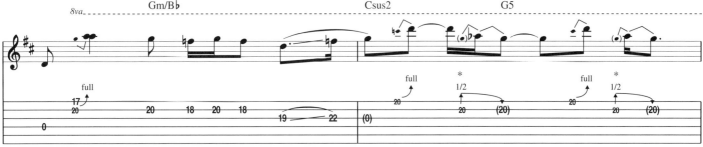

*Pre-bend is result of previously bent higher string

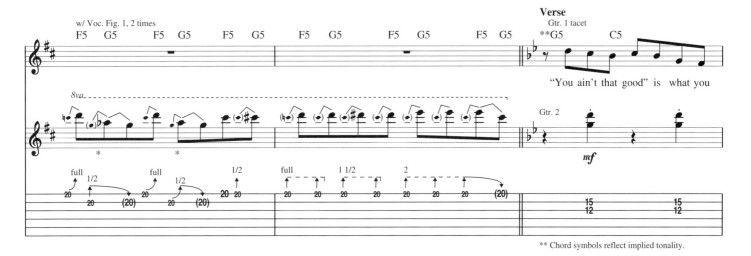

**Chord symbols reflect implied tonality.

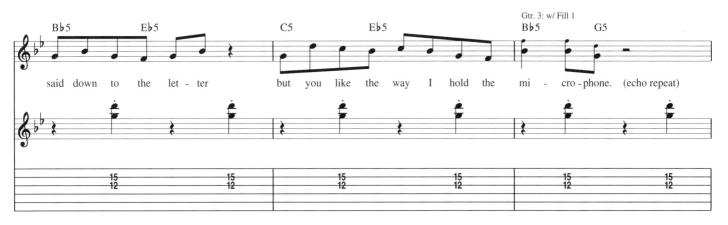

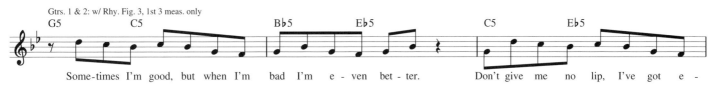

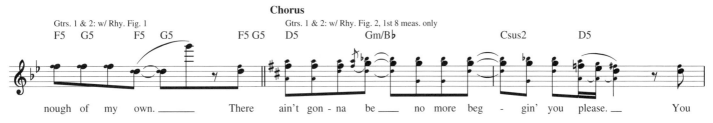

Pink

Words and Music by Tyler/Supa/Ballard

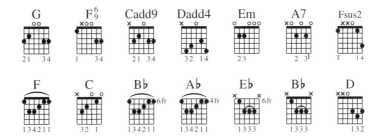

Gtr. 5; Open G Tuning:

① = D   ④ = D
② = B   ⑤ = G
③ = G   ⑥ = D

Intro

Moderately Slow Rock ♩ = 88

Verse

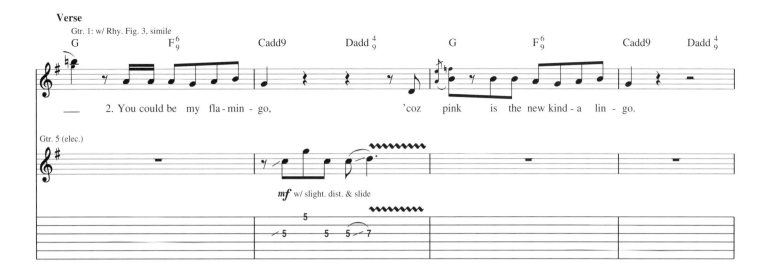

2. You could be my fla-min-go, 'coz pink is the new kind-a lin-go.

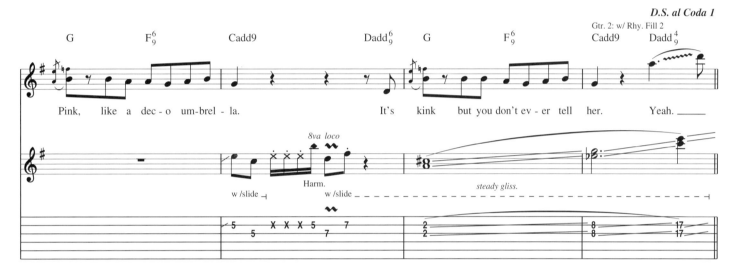

D.S. al Coda 1

Pink, like a dec-o um-brel-la. It's kink but you don't ev-er tell her. Yeah.____

⊕ *Coda 1*

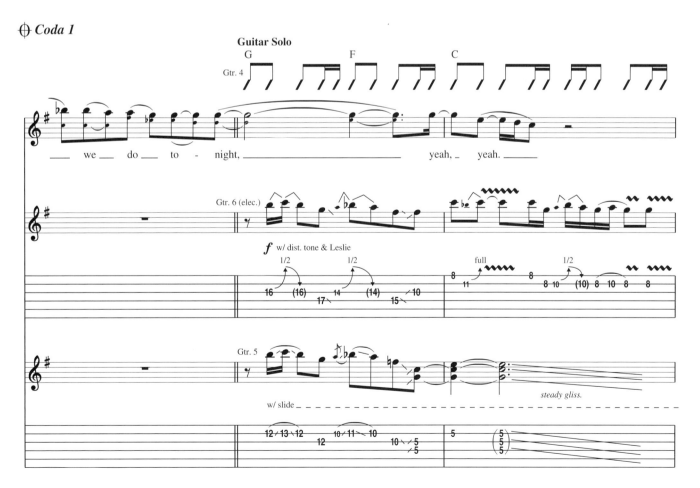

Guitar Solo

____ we do to - night,____ yeah,__ yeah.____

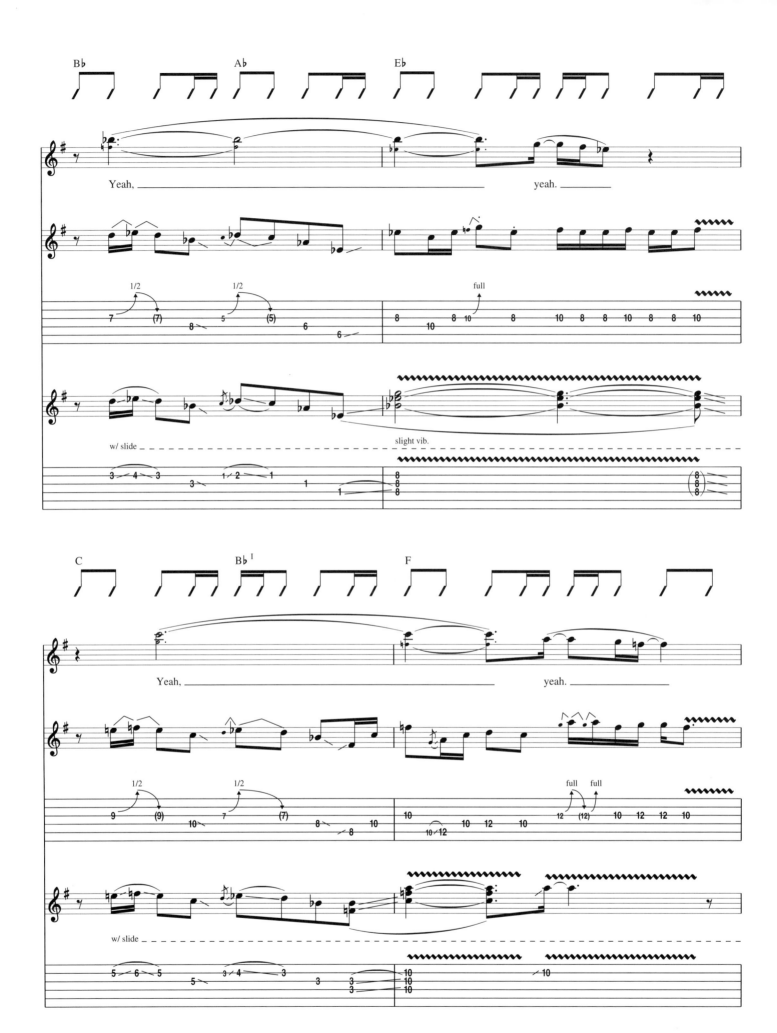

I Don't Want to Miss a Thing

from the Touchstone Picture ARMAGEDDON

Words and Music by Diane Warren

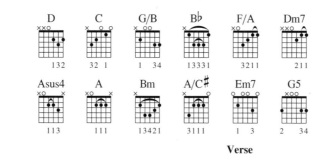

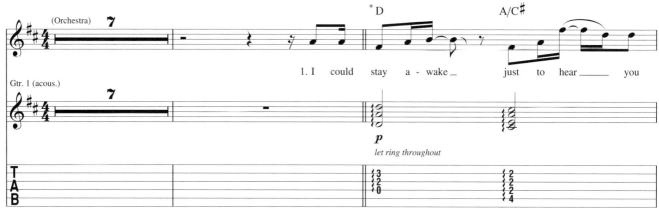

Intro
Slowly ♩ = 60

Verse

*Chord symbols reflect overall harmony.

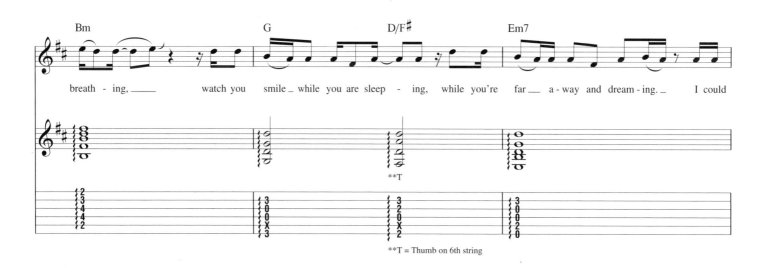

**T = Thumb on 6th string

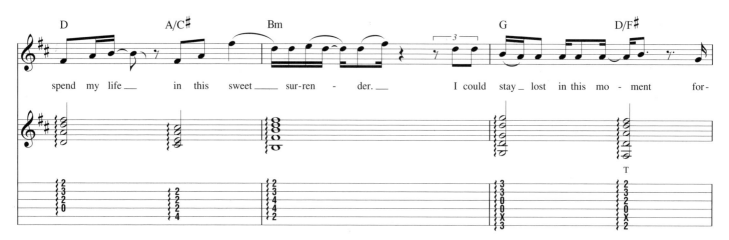

the sweet-est dream would nev - er do.___ I'd still_____ miss you, ba - by, and I don't want to miss a thing.___
dream.)

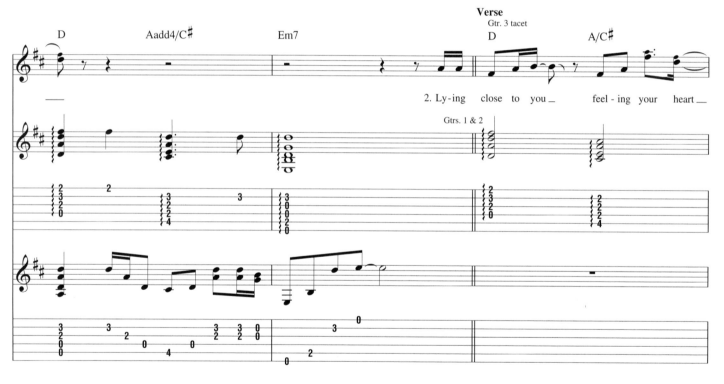

2. Ly-ing close to you ___ feel-ing your heart ___

___ beat - ing ___ and I'm won-d'ring what you're dream - ing, won-d'ring if it's me you're see - ing. Then I

228

kiss your eyes ____ and thank God we're to - geth - er. ____ I just want to

stay with you in this mo - ment for - ev - er, ____ for - ev - er, and ev - er. _____

Chorus
Gtrs. 1 & 2: w/ Rhy Fig. 1
Gtr. 3: w/ Rhy. Fig. 1A

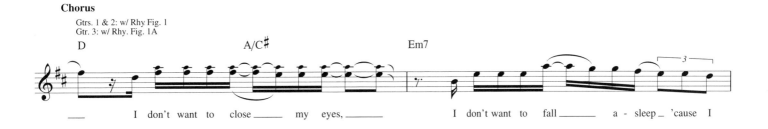

____ I don't want to close ____ my eyes, ____ I don't want to fall ____ a - sleep __ 'cause I

Bkgd. Voc.: w/ Voc. Fig. 1

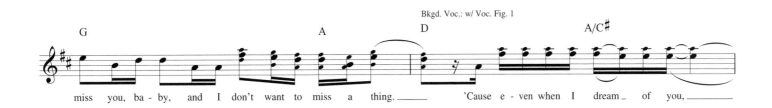

miss you, ba - by, and I don't want to miss a thing. ____ 'Cause e - ven when I dream __ of you, ____

the sweet - est dream would nev - er do. __ I'd still ____ miss you ba - by, and I don't want to miss a thing. ____

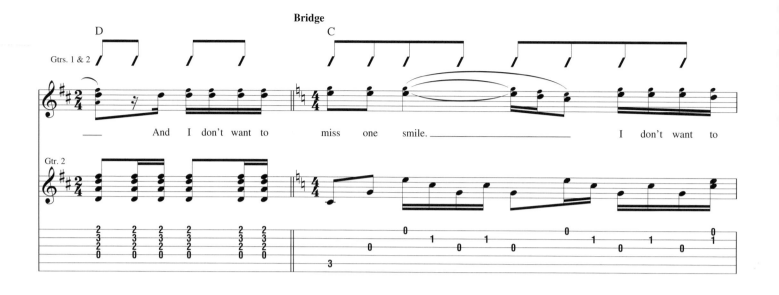

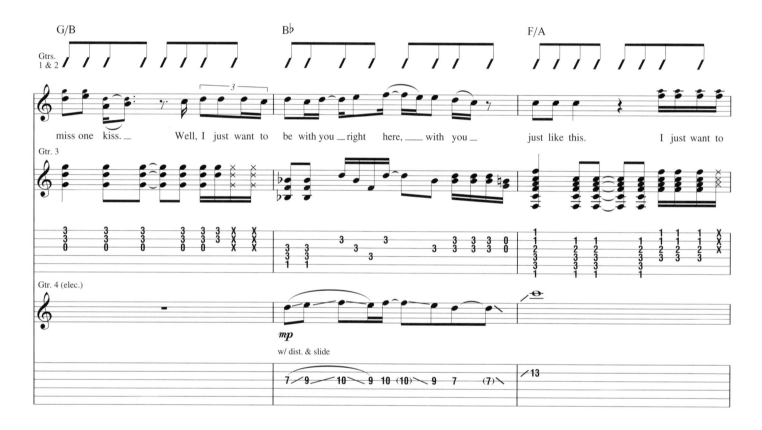

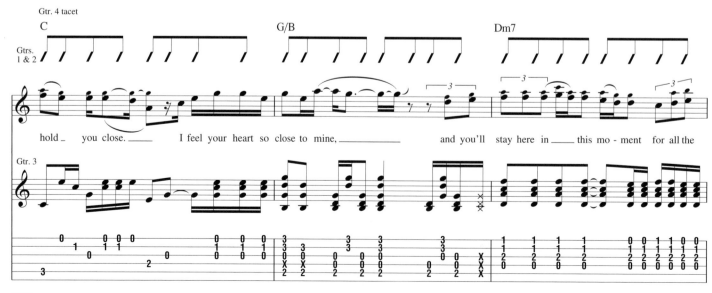

Chorus
Gtrs. 1 & 2: w/ Rhy. Fig. 1 (1 1/2 times)
Gtr. 3: w/ Rhy. Fig. 1A (1 1/2 times)

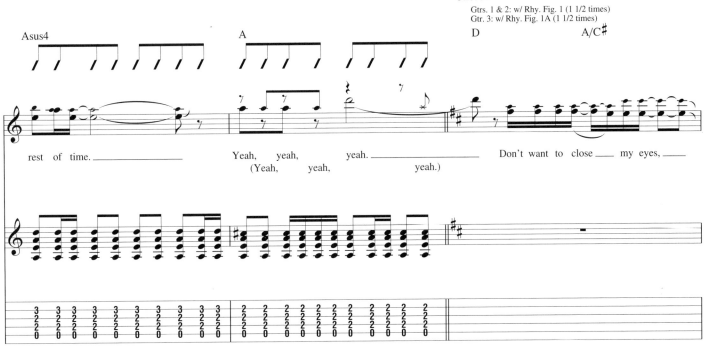

rest of time. _____ Yeah, yeah, yeah. _____ Don't want to close ___ my eyes, ___
(Yeah, yeah, yeah.)

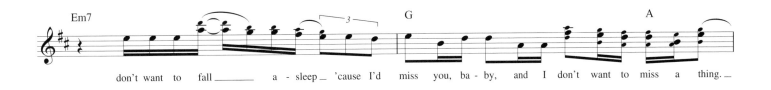

don't want to fall _____ a - sleep ___ 'cause I'd miss you, ba - by, and I don't want to miss a thing. ___

Bkgd. Voc.: w/ Voc. Fig. 1

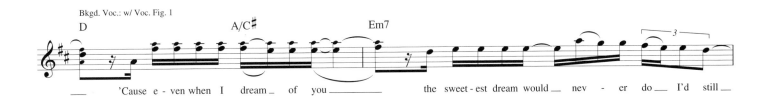

___ 'Cause e - ven when I dream ___ of you _____ the sweet - est dream would ___ nev - er do ___ I'd still ___

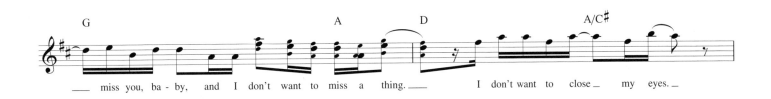

___ miss you, ba - by, and I don't want to miss a thing. ___ I don't want to close ___ my eyes. ___

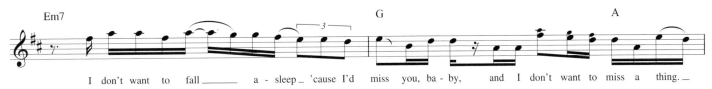

I don't want to fall _____ a - sleep ___ 'cause I'd miss you, ba - by, and I don't want to miss a thing. ___

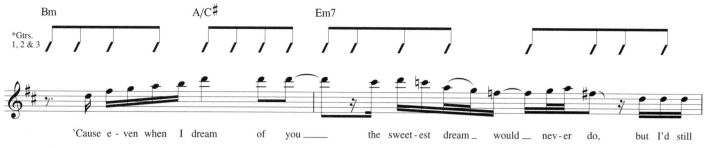

'Cause e - ven when I dream of you _____ the sweet-est dream _ would _ nev-er do, but I'd still

*Composite arrangement

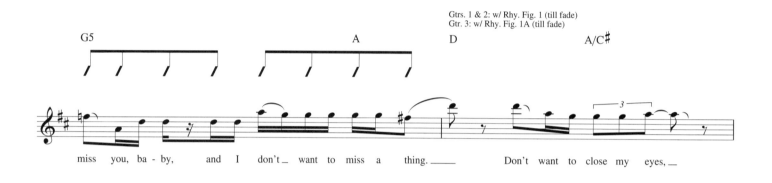

miss you, ba - by, and I don't _ want to miss a thing. _____ Don't want to close my eyes, _

I don't want to fall _____ a - sleep, _____ yeah, and I don't want to miss a thing.

Outro

Begin fade

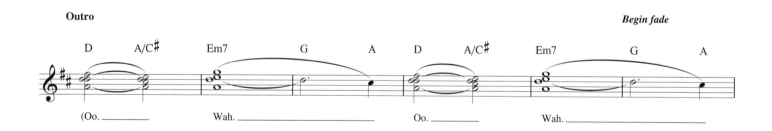

(Oo. _____ Wah. _____ Oo. _____ Wah. _____

Fade out

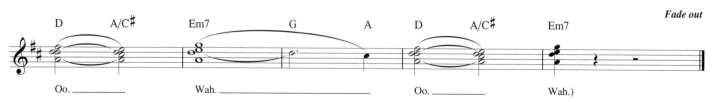

Oo. _____ Wah. _____ Oo. _____ Wah.)

Jaded

Words and Music by Tyler/Frederiksen

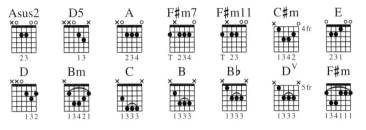

Tune up 1/4 step

Intro

Moderate Rock ♩ = 120

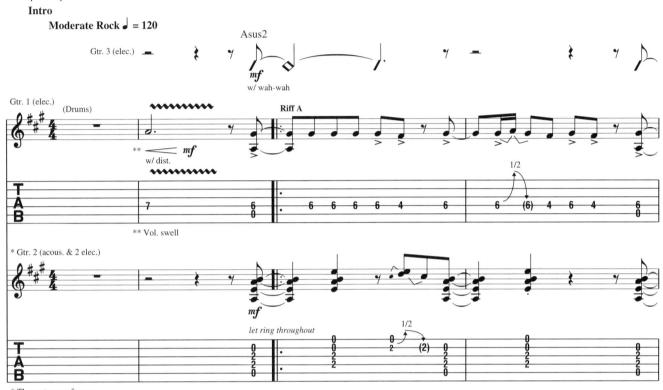

* Three gtrs. arr. for one.

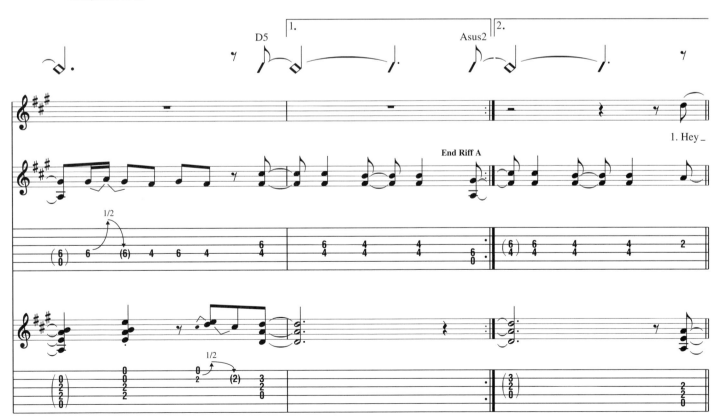

Verse

Gtr. 3 tacet
2nd time, Gtr. 1: w/ Fill 1

Gtr. 1 tacet

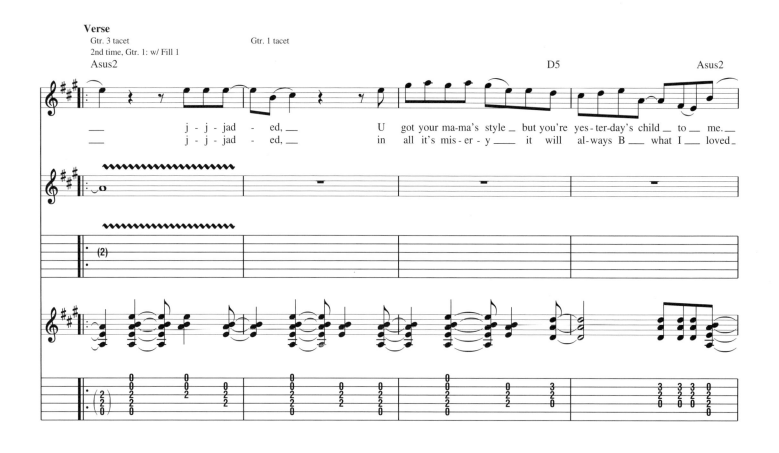

j - j - jad - ed, __ U got your ma-ma's style __ but you're yes-ter-day's child __ to __ me.
j - j - jad - ed, __ in all it's mis-er - y __ it will al-ways B __ what I __ loved __

So jad - ed, __ U think that's where it's at __ but is that where it's spos - ta B? __
and hat - ed. __ And may - be take a ride __ to the oth - er side we're think-in'

w/ amp
tremolo

Fill 1
Gtr. 1

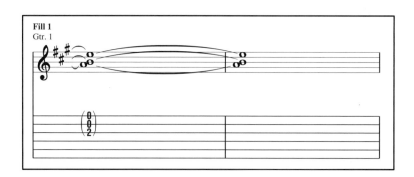

234

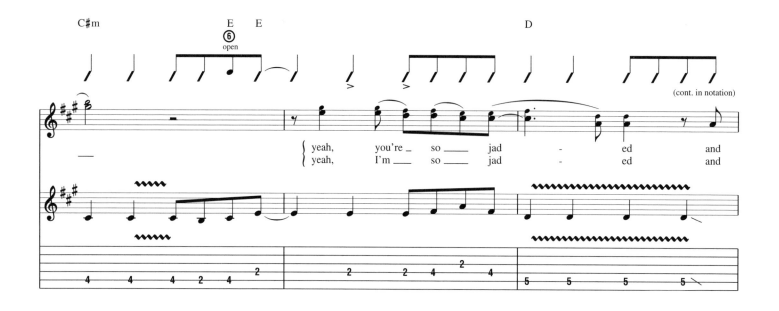

yeah, you're _ so _____ jad - ed and
yeah, I'm _____ so _____ jad - ed and

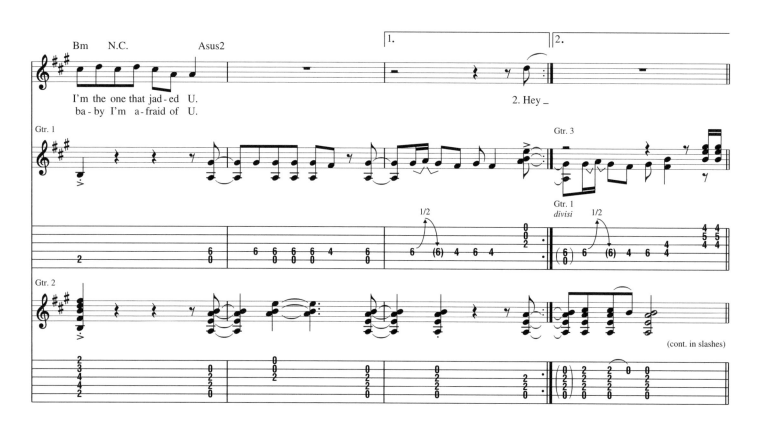

I'm the one that jad - ed U.
ba - by I'm a - fraid of U.

2. Hey _

Bridge

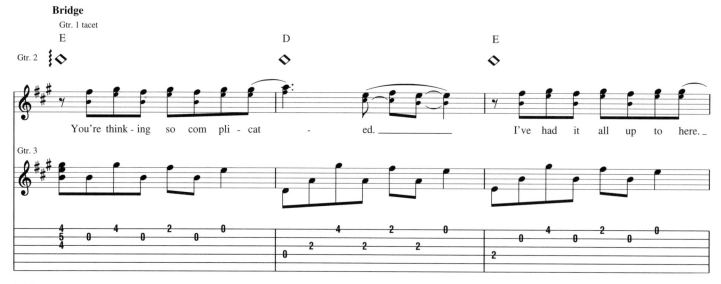

You're think - ing so com pli - cat - ed. _____ I've had it all up to here. _

But it's so o-ver-rat - ed.___ Luv and hate___

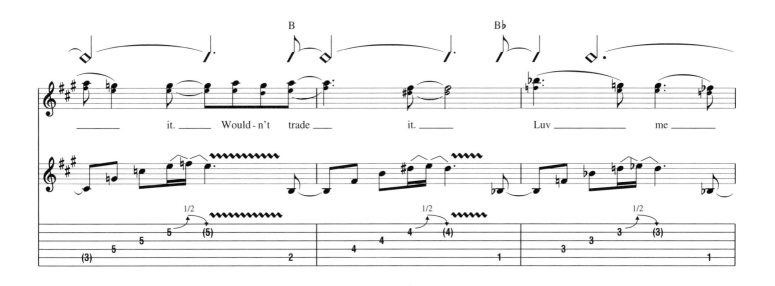

it.___ Would-n't trade___ it.___ Luv_____ me_____

Guitar Solo

Gtr. 1: w/ Riff A

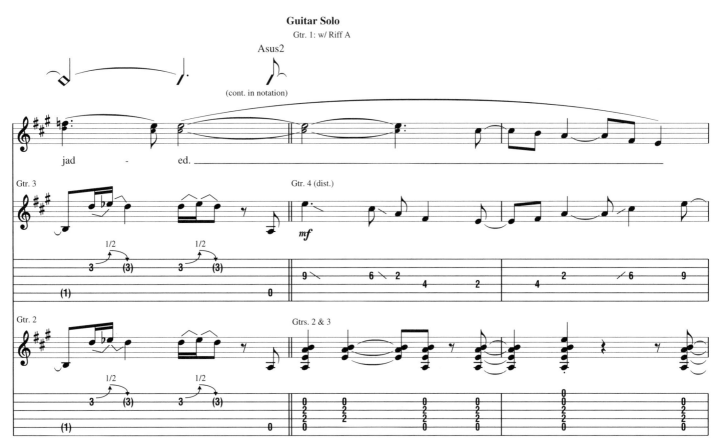

jad - ed._____

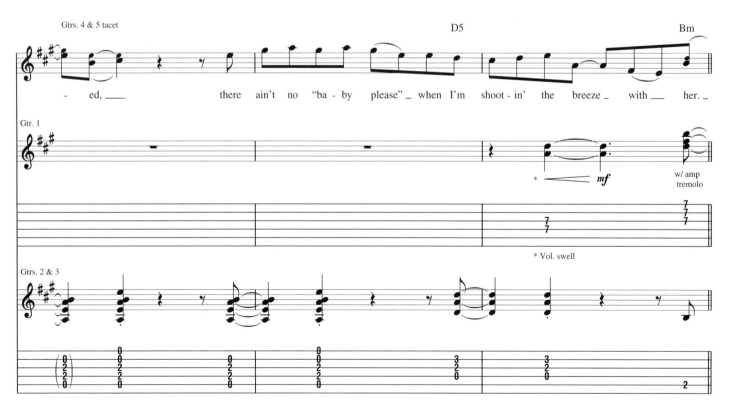

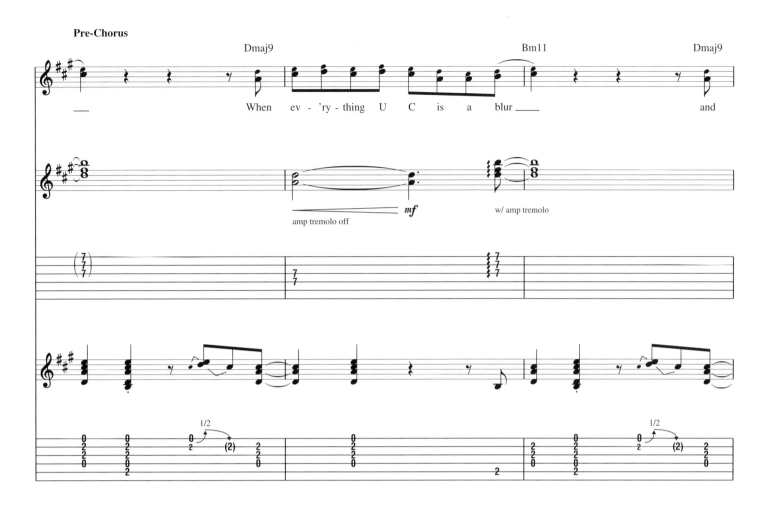

When ev - 'ry-thing U C is a blur ____ and

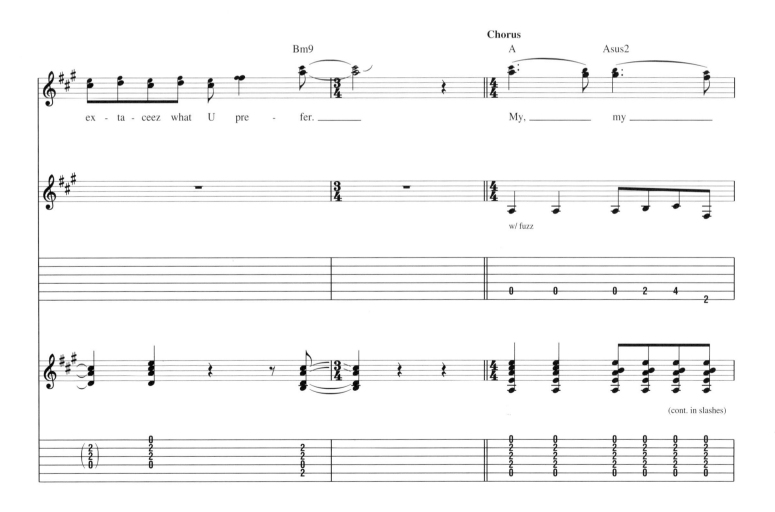

ex - ta - ceez what U pre - fer. ____ My, ____ my ____

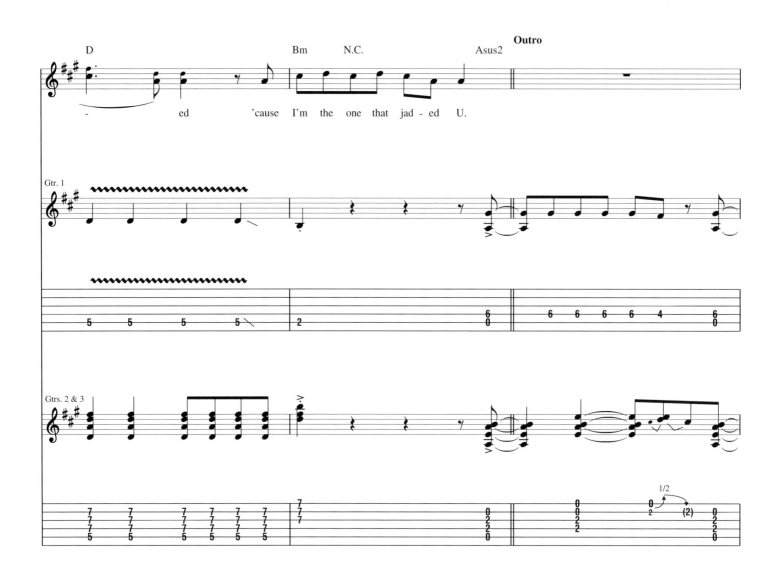

ed   'cause I'm the one that jad - ed U.

Just Push Play

Words and Music by Tyler/Hudson/Dudas

go - in dimm mon ya. Mih go - in dimm mon ya.

U all up in de Kool-aid but you do not know de fla - vor.

Hen me did de yo na. It's Mis - ter him that done that Ka

Get in - to the zone, bay-bee, and do your-self a fa - vor.

Pre-Chorus

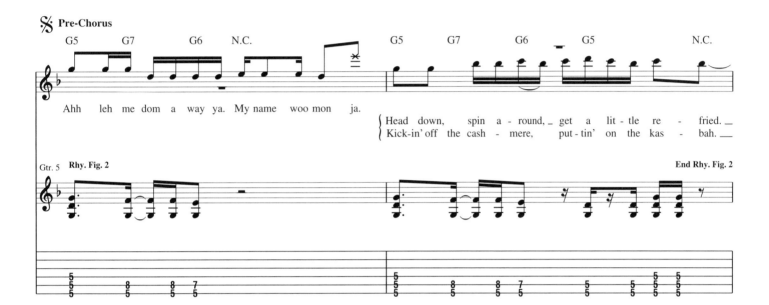

Ahh leh me dom a way ya. My name woo mon ja.

Head down, spin a - round, _ get a lit - tle re - fried. _

Kick-in' off the cash - mere, put - tin' on the kas - bah. _

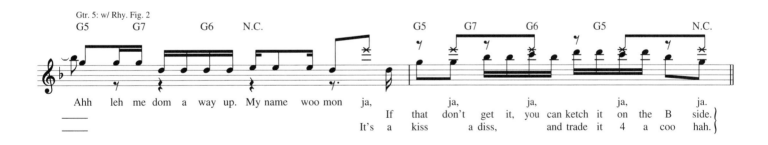

Ahh leh me dom a way up. My name woo mon ja, ja, ja, ja, ja.

If that don't get it, you can ketch it on the B side.

It's a kiss a diss, and trade it 4 a coo hah.

Chorus

1st time, Gtrs. 5 & 6: w/ Riff B (2 times)
2nd time, Gtrs. 5 & 6: w/ Riff B (1 1/2 times)

(Just push play.

F N A. ___

Just push play.

They're gon - na bleep it an - y - way.

* Studio scratching effect

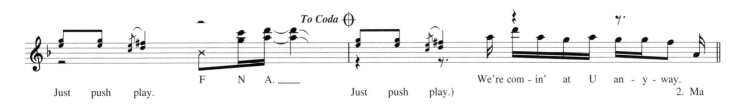

Just push play.

F N A. ___

Just push play.)

We're com - in' at U an - y - way.

2. Ma

Gtrs. 5 & 6: w/ Rhy. Fig. 1 (2 times)

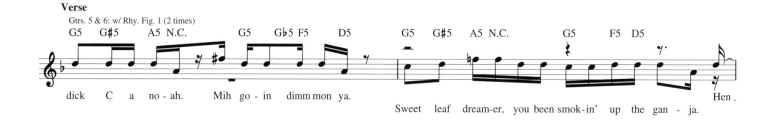

dick C a no - ah. Mih go - in dimm mon ya.

Sweet leaf dream-er, you been smok-in' up the gan - ja.

Hen -

D.S. al Coda

____ me did de yo na. It's Mis - ter him that done that Ka.

Damned if U do, yeah, but don't get an - y on ya.

Coda

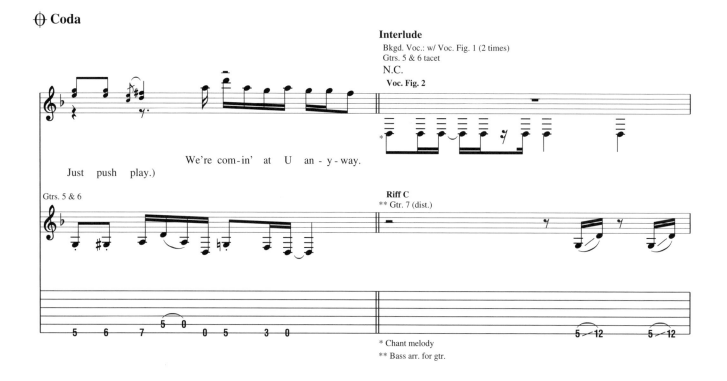

Interlude

Bkgd. Voc.: w/ Voc. Fig. 1 (2 times)
Gtrs. 5 & 6 tacet

N.C.

Voc. Fig. 2

We're com-in' at U an - y - way.

Just push play.)

Gtrs. 5 & 6

Riff C

** Gtr. 7 (dist.)

* Chant melody
** Bass arr. for gtr.

Gtr. 7: w/ Riff C

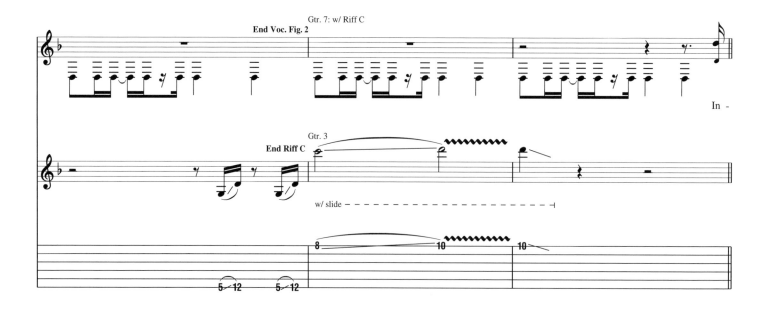

End Voc. Fig. 2

In -

Gtr. 3

End Riff C

w/ slide -- -- -- -- -- -- -- -- -- --

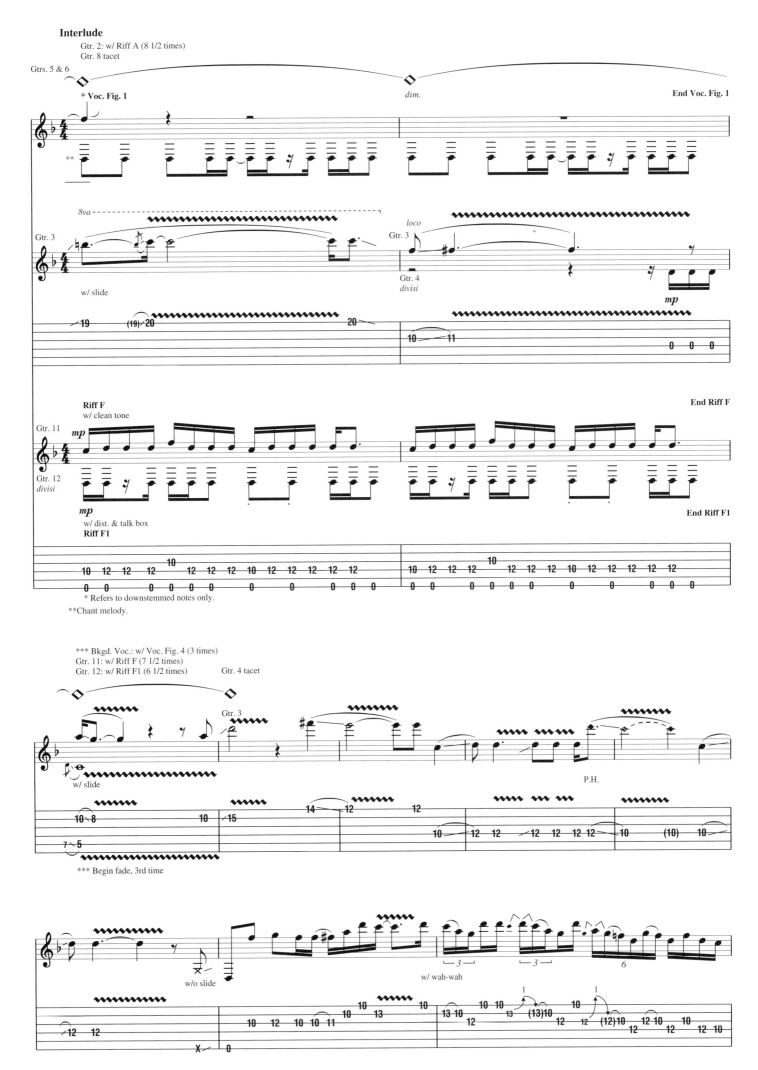

Walk This Way

Words and Music by Tyler/Perry

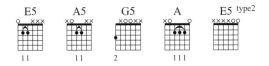

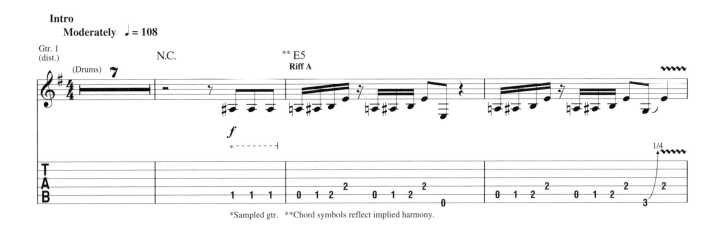

*Sampled gtr. **Chord symbols reflect implied harmony.

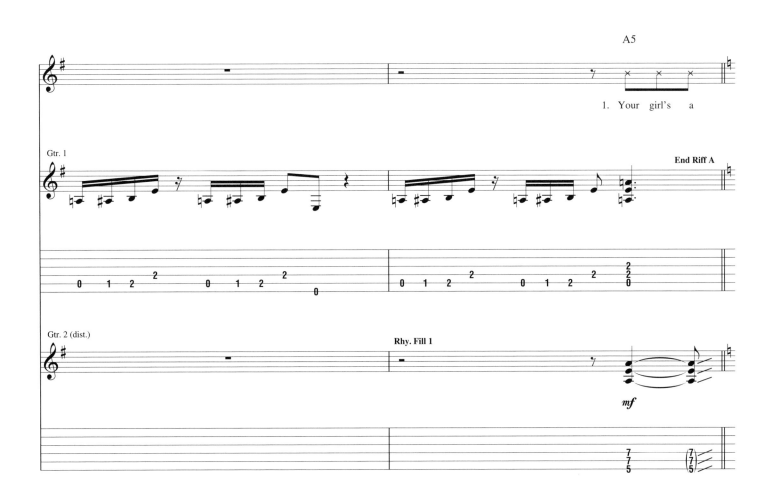

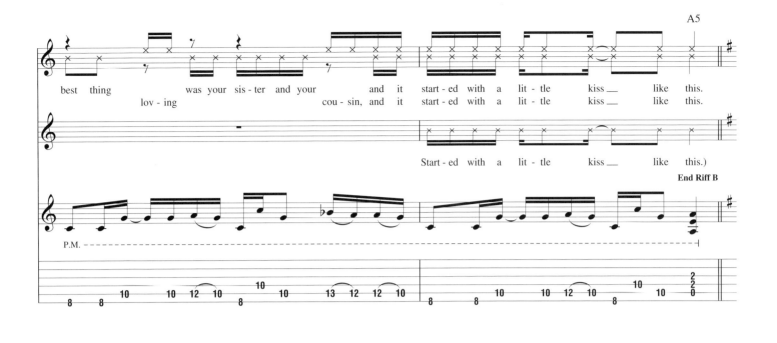

Interlude
Gtr. 1: w/ Riff A
Gtr. 2: w/ Rhy. Fill 1

Verse
Gtr. 1: w/ Riff B (1st 6 meas.)

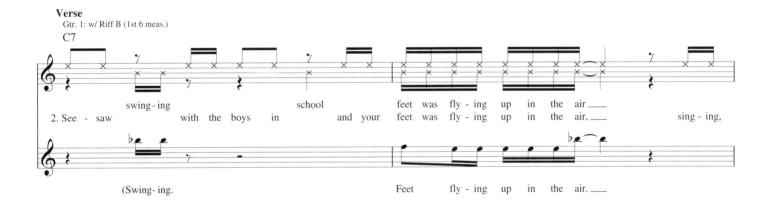

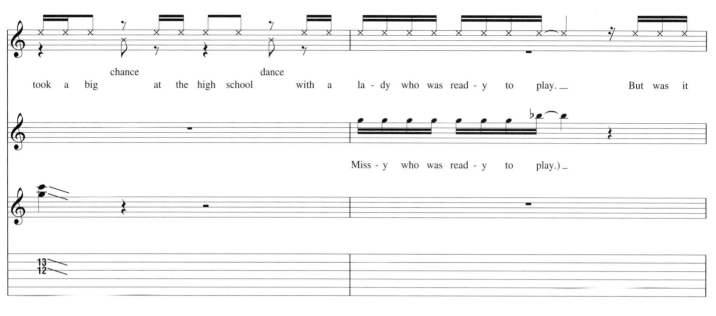

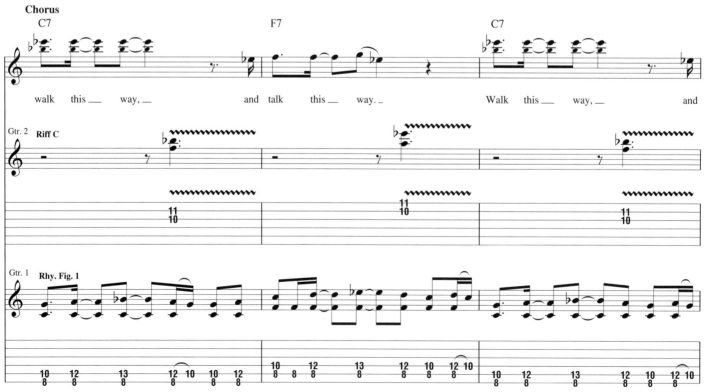

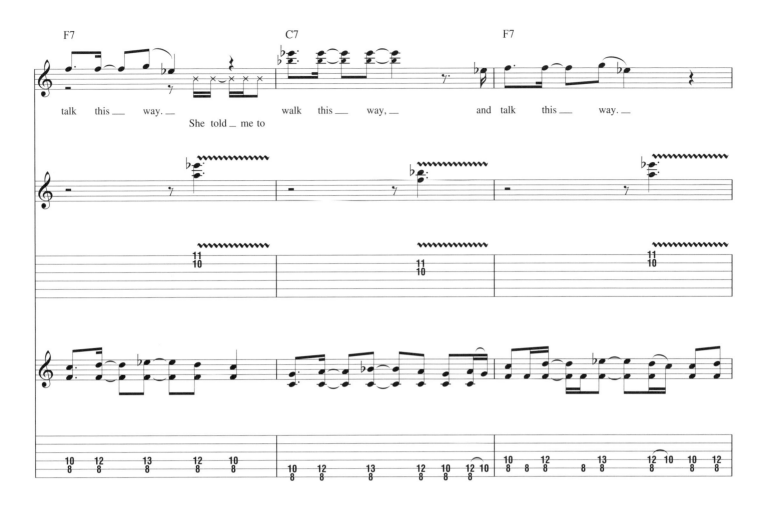

talk this __ way. __   walk this __ way, __   and talk this __ way. __

She told __ me to

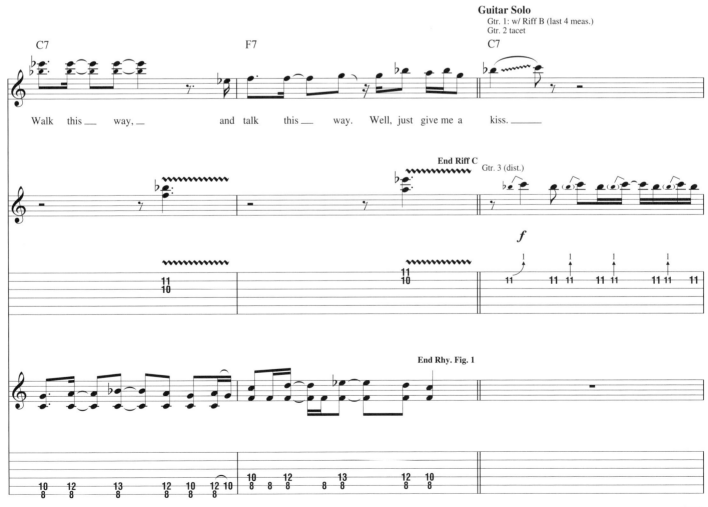

Walk this __ way, __   and talk this __ way. Well, just give me a   kiss. _____

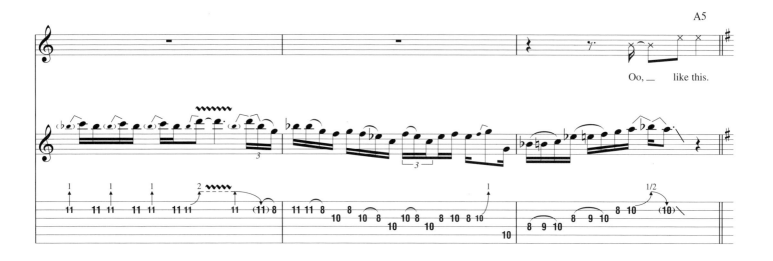

Oo, __ like this.

Interlude

Gtr. 1: w/ Riff A
Gtr. 3 tacet

E5

Verse

A5   N.C. (C7)

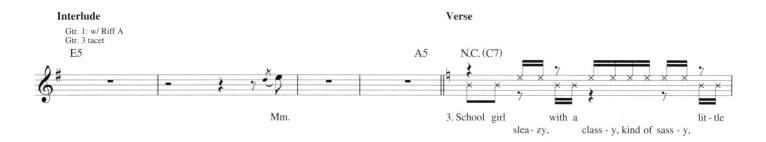

Mm.

3. School girl   with a   lit - tle
slea - zy,   class - y, kind of sass - y,

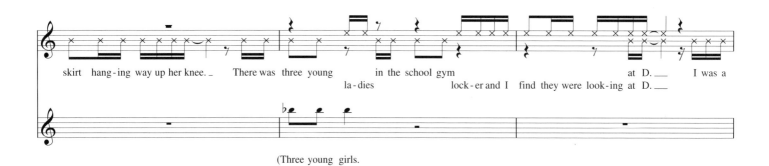

skirt hang-ing way up her knee. __ There was three young   in the school gym   at D. __   I was a
la - dies   lock-er and I   find they were look-ing at D. __

(Three young girls.

high school   nev-er made it with a   till the boys told   Then my next   door   with a daugh-ter had a fav-or and I
los - er,   la - dy   told me some-thing I missed. _   neigh-bor   fav-or

Los - er,   with a,   till the,   told me,   missed. _   Door,   had a daugh-ter,   fav-or,

Gtr. 1

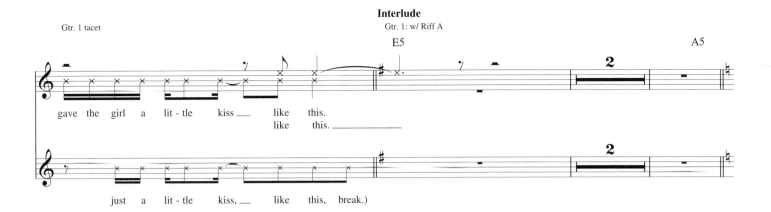

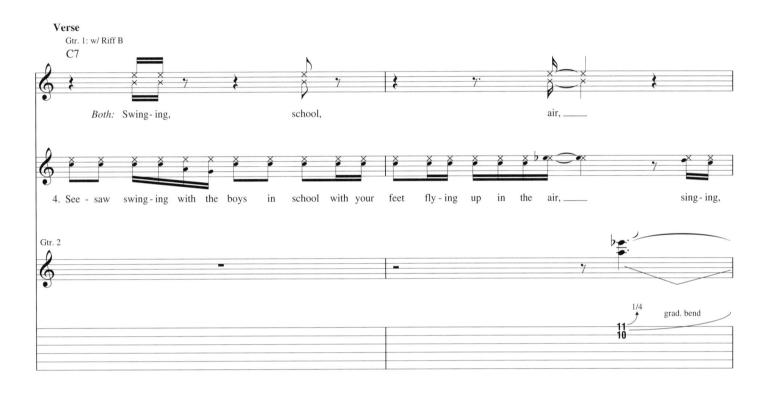

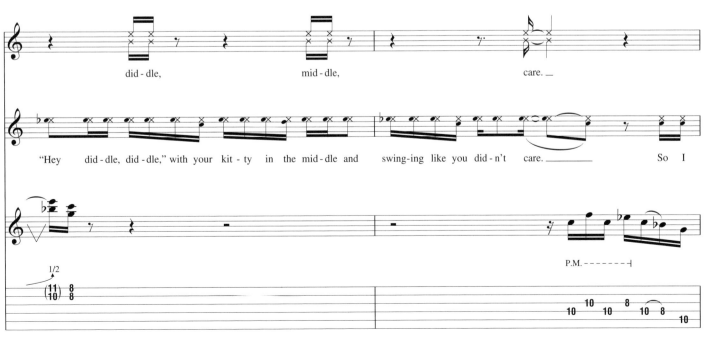

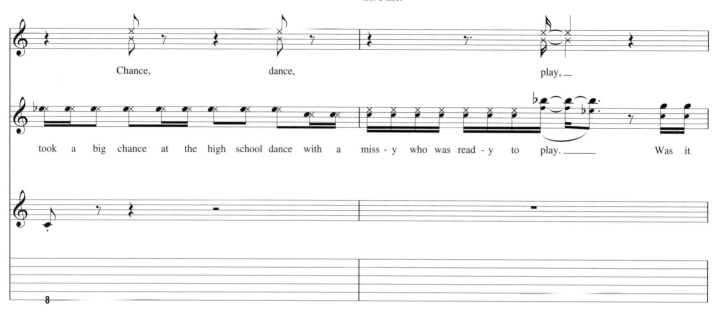

Chance, dance, play, ____

took a big chance at the high school dance with a miss-y who was read-y to play. ____ Was it

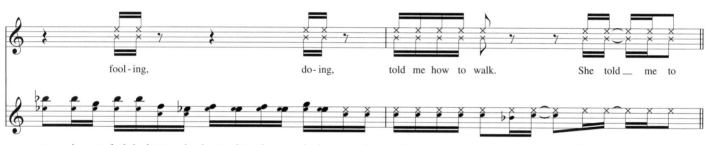

fool-ing, do-ing, told me how to walk. She told ___ me to

me she was fool-ing 'cause she knew what she was do-ing when she told me how to walk this way? ___ She told ___ me to

Chorus
Gtr. 1: w/ Rhy. Fig. 1
Gtr. 2: w/ Riff C

C7   F7   C7

walk this ___ way ___ and talk this ___ way. ___ Walk this ___ way ___ and

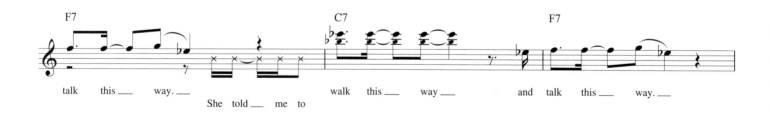

F7   C7   F7

talk this ___ way. ___ walk this ___ way ___ and talk this ___ way. ___
         She told ___ me to

C7   F7

Walk this ___ way ___ and talk this ___ way. Well, just give me some
                                           (Ah, ah, ah, ah,

Interlude

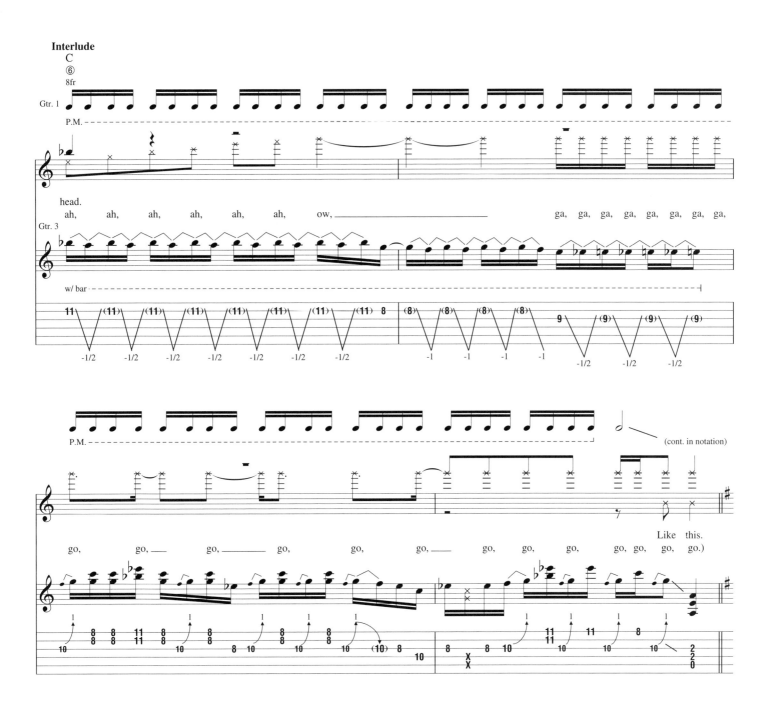

Outro - Guitar Solo

Gtr. 1: w/ Rhy. Fig. 2 (11 times)
Gtr. 2: w/ Rhy. Fig. 2A (4 1/2 times)

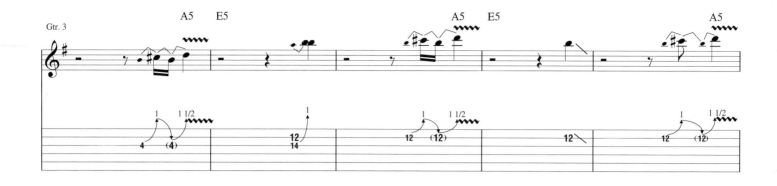

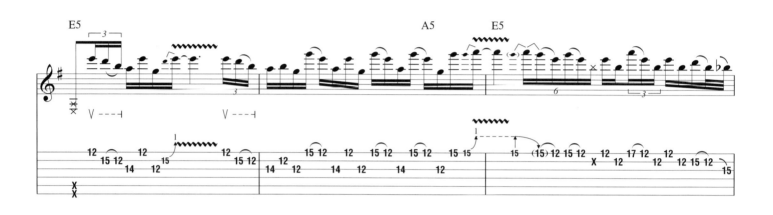

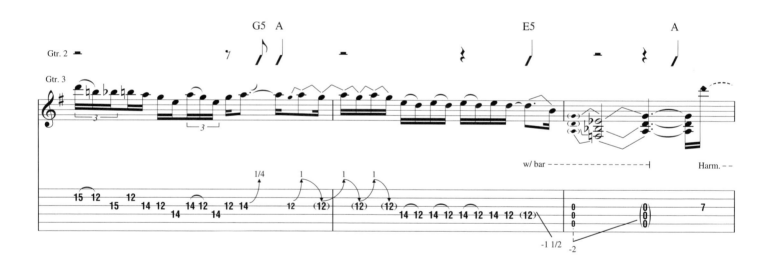

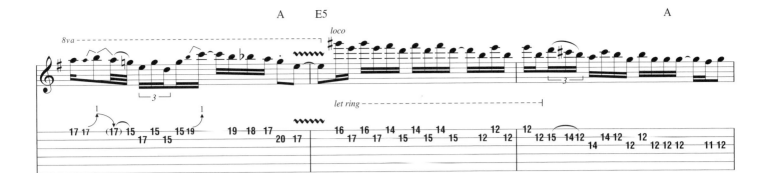

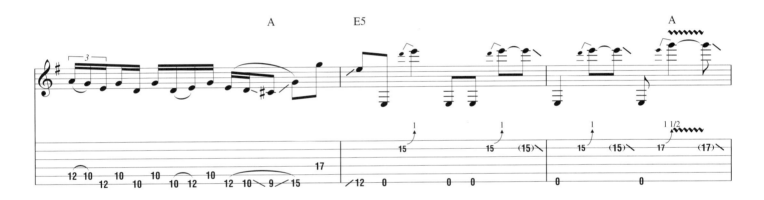

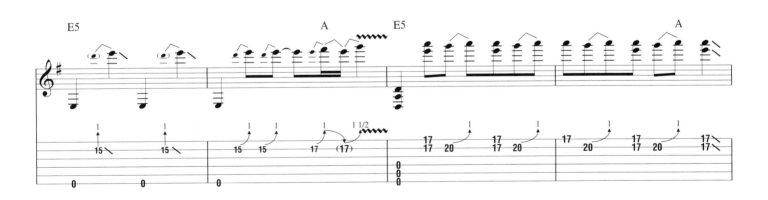

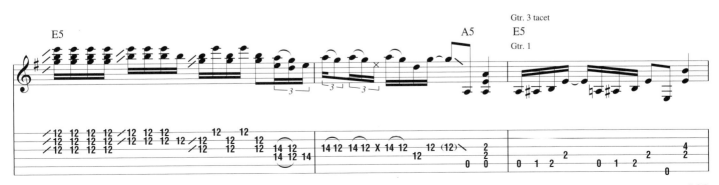

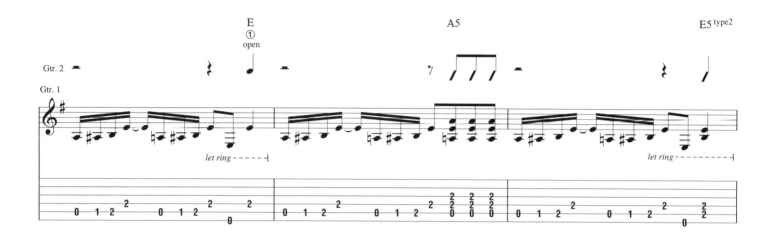

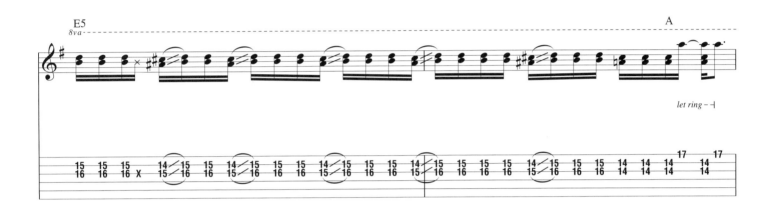

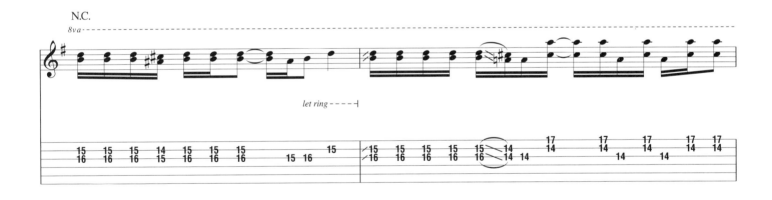

Girls of Summer

Words and Music by Tyler/Perry/Frederiksen

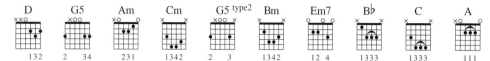

Gtr. 6: Drop D tuning:
(low to high) D-A-D-G-B-E
Gtr. 7: Open G tuning:
(low to high) D-G-D-G-B-D

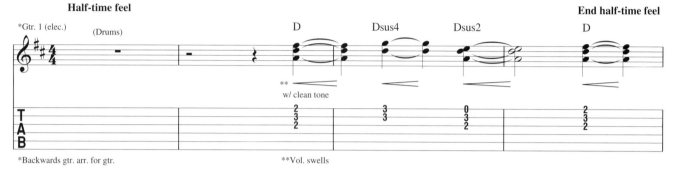

*Backwards gtr. arr. for gtr.   **Vol. swells

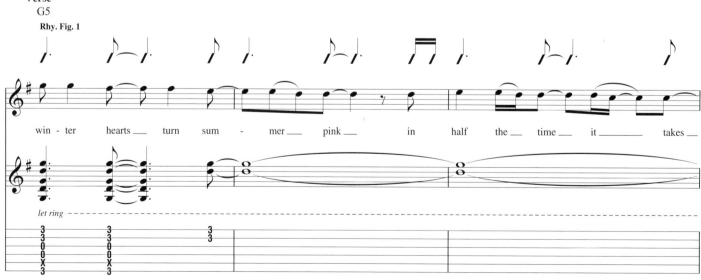

like that _you can't go wrong about the girls of sum-_

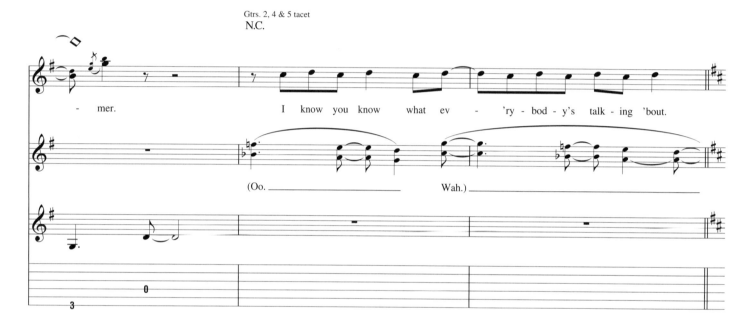

-mer. _I know you know what ev - 'ry - bod - y's talk - ing 'bout._

(Oo. _____ Wah.) _____

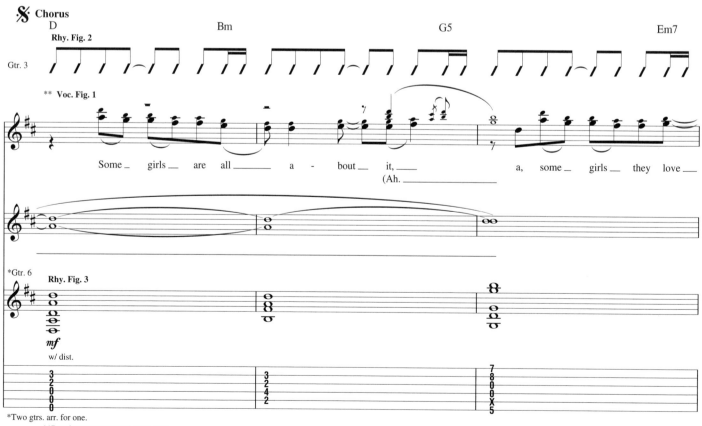

§ **Chorus**

Some girls are all about it, _a, some girls they love_

(Ah. _____

*Two gtrs. arr. for one.

**Pertains to upstemmed notes only.

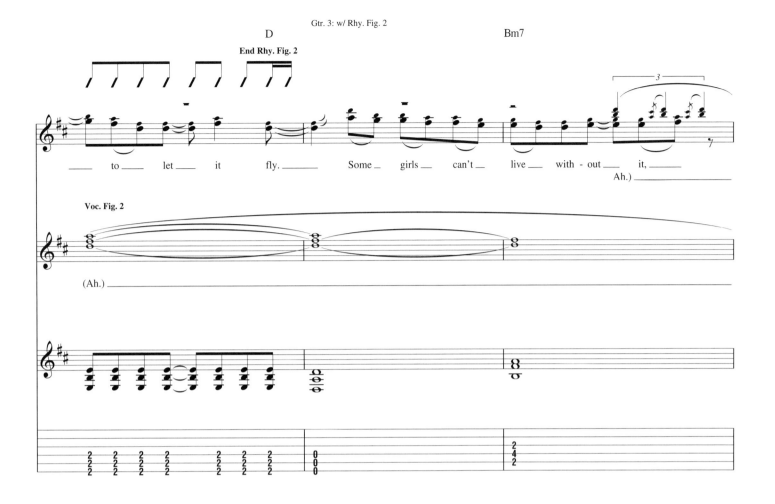

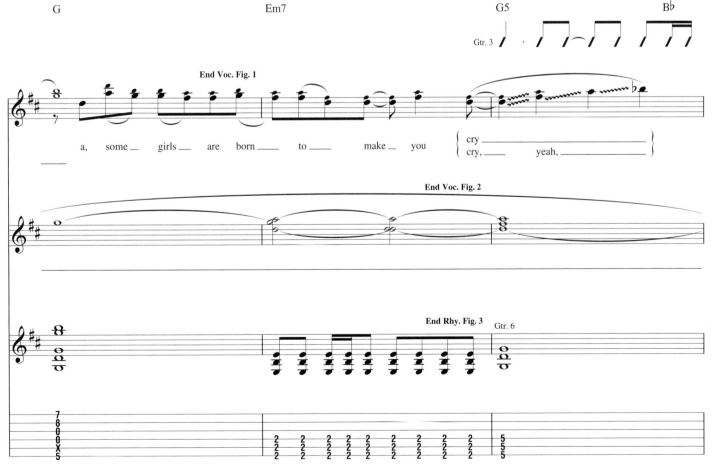

the girls of summer. A, do you know what ev - 'ry-bod-y's talk-ing 'bout?

(Oo. Wah.)

Yeah, yeah, yeah, yeah. They get you climb - ing the walls,

they get you caught in their spell. They get you speak-ing in tongues. Could this be heav-en or hell?

To fall in love twice a day is such a sweet price to pay.

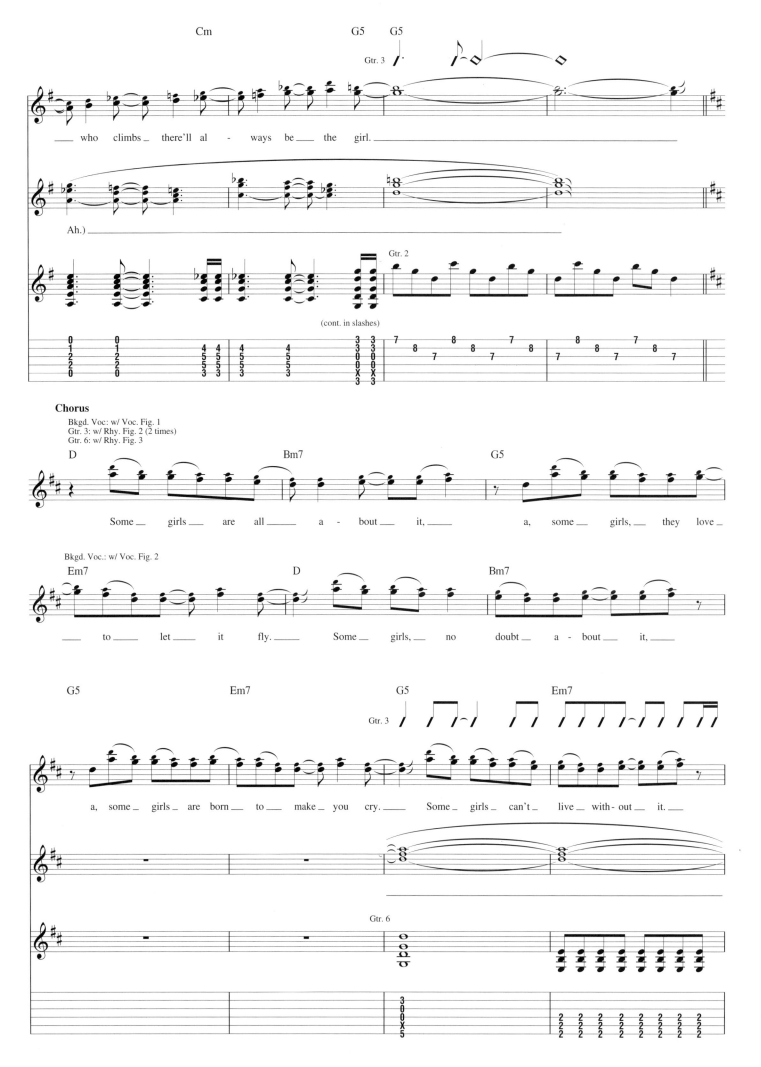

who climbs there'll al - ways be the girl.

Ah.)

(cont. in slashes)

Chorus
Bkgd. Voc: w/ Voc. Fig. 1
Gtr. 3: w/ Rhy. Fig. 2 (2 times)
Gtr. 6: w/ Rhy. Fig. 3

Some girls are all a - bout it, a, some girls, they love

Bkgd. Voc.: w/ Voc. Fig. 2

to let it fly. Some girls, no doubt a - bout it,

a, some girls are born to make you cry. Some girls can't live with - out it.

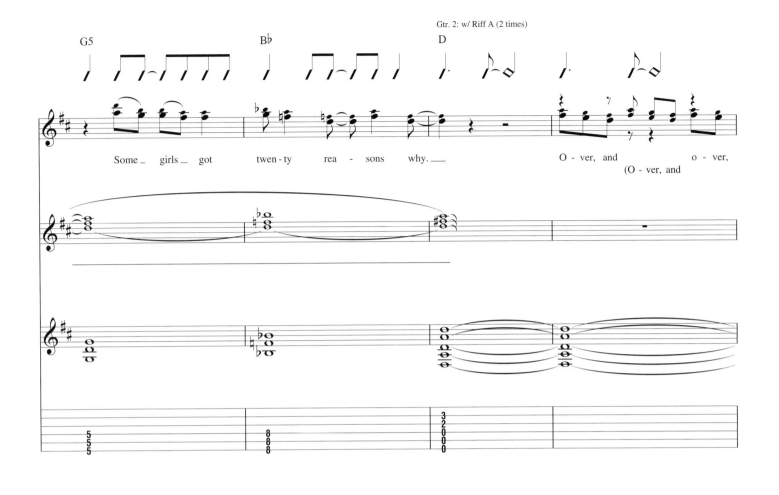

Gtr. 2: w/ Riff A (2 times)

Some girls got twen-ty rea-sons why. ___ O-ver, and o-ver,
(O-ver, and

and o-ver, and.
o-ver, and o-ver, and...)

Gtr. 8 (elec.)

𝆑
w/ dist. & slide

Gtr. 6

Lay It Down

Words and Music by Tyler/Perry/Frederiksen/De Grate

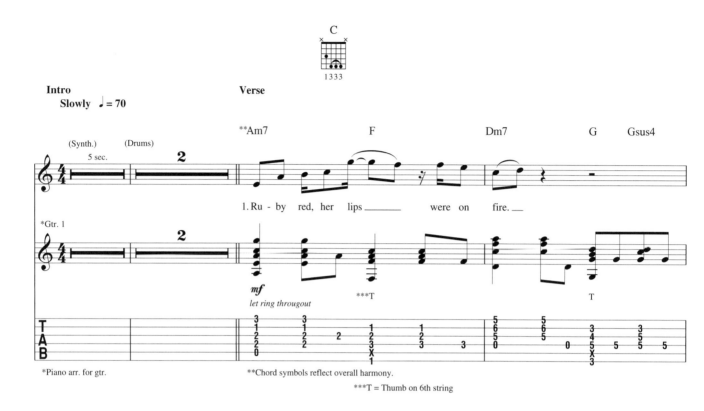

love__ you__ want,__ then__ you__ won't__ mind a lit-tle ten - der - ness__ that some-times is so hard to find.__ (Lay it __

%: **Chorus**

Lay it down,__ make it all _____ right.__ Lay it down,__ I'll hold you

down. _____ Lay it down. _____

Gtr. 3
(elec.) **Riff A1**

mp
w/ clean tone & heavy tremolo
let ring throughout

*Gtr. 2
(elec.) **Riff A**

mp
w/ clean tone
let ring throughout

*Two gtrs. arr. for one.

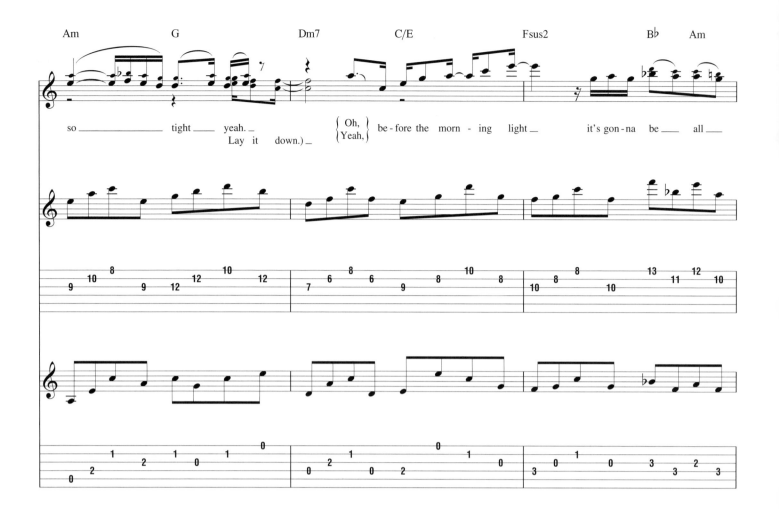

so _____ tight _____ yeah. _____
Lay it down.) _
{ Oh, }
{ Yeah, } be - fore the morn - ing light _____ it's gon - na be _____ all _____

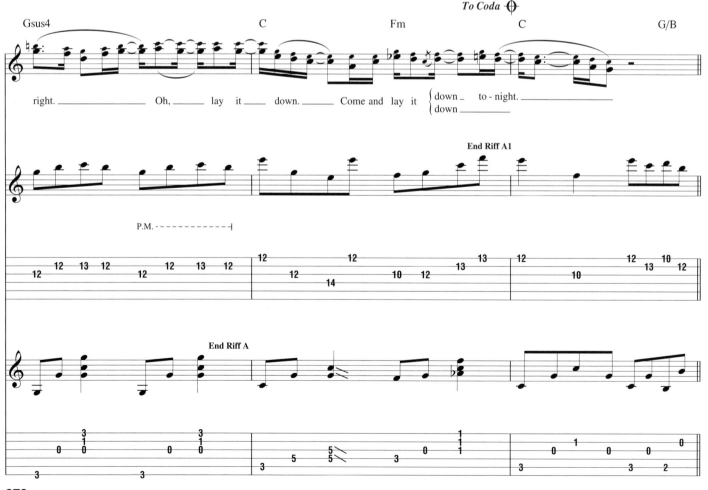

To Coda ⊕

right. _____ Oh, _____ lay it _____ down. _____ Come and lay it { down _ to - night. _____
{ down _____

End Riff A1

P.M. - - - - - - - - - ┤

End Riff A

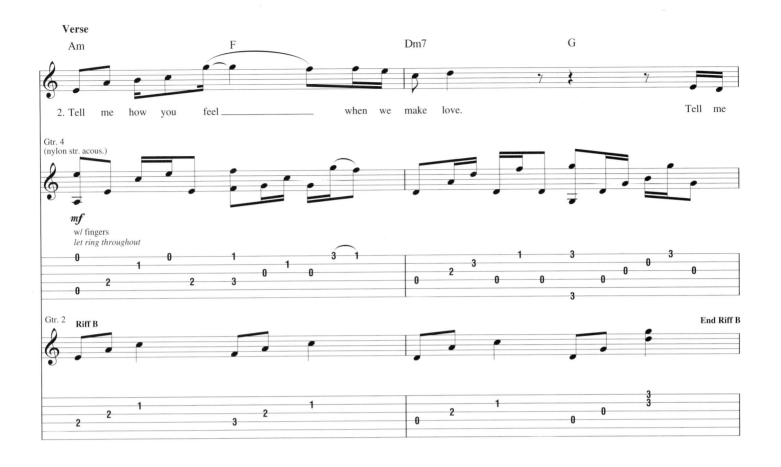

Verse

2. Tell me how you feel _____ when we make love. Tell me

Gtr. 4
(nylon str. acous.)

mf
w/ fingers
let ring throughout

Gtr. 2 **Riff B**

End Riff B

Gtr. 2: w/ Riff B (2 times)

is it real ___ or just _____ make be - lieve? _____

Gtr. 4

You will nev - er know _____ what you're made of till you

o - pen up your heart _____ to re - ceive. _____ 'Cause if the love _ you _ got's _ that _

D.S. al Coda

same _ old _ grind, we're talk - ing ten - der-ness that's so hard to find and I'm here to re - mind you.
(Lay it _____

⊕ Coda

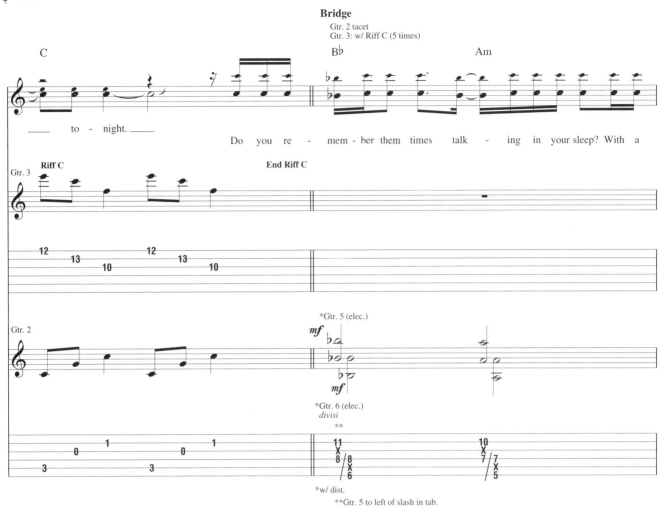

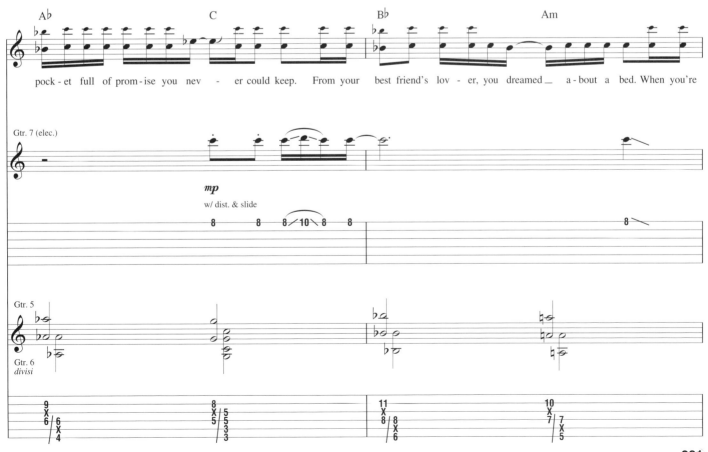

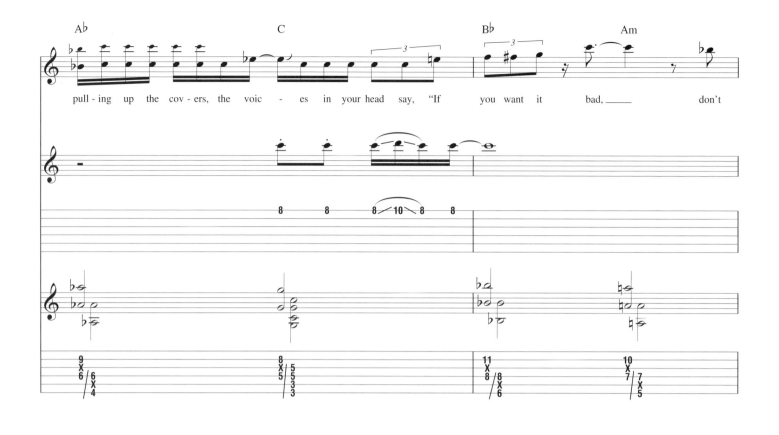

pull - ing up the cov - ers, the voic - es in your head say, "If   you want it   bad, ____   don't

ev - er let it slip a - way." ____   'Cause if it's love ____ you ____ want ____ and   ten - der - ness,

(Lay it ____ down ____

Guitar Notation Legend

Guitar Music can be notated three different ways: on a *musical staff*, in *tablature*, and in *rhythm slashes*.

RHYTHM SLASHES are written above the staff. Strum chords in the rhythm indicated. Use the chord diagrams found at the top of the first page of the transcription for the appropriate chord voicings. Round noteheads indicate single notes.

THE MUSICAL STAFF shows pitches and rhythms and is divided by bar lines into measures. Pitches are named after the first seven letters of the alphabet.

TABLATURE graphically represents the guitar fingerboard. Each horizontal line represents a a string, and each number represents a fret.

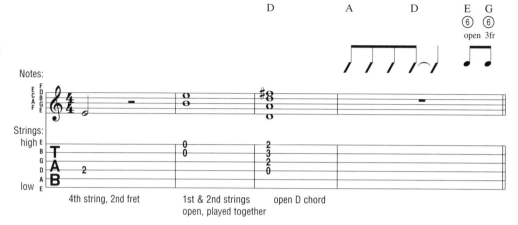

4th string, 2nd fret · 1st & 2nd strings open, played together · open D chord

Definitions for Special Guitar Notation

HALF-STEP BEND: Strike the note and bend up 1/2 step.

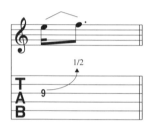

WHOLE-STEP BEND: Strike the note and bend up one step.

GRACE NOTE BEND: Strike the note and immediately bend up as indicated.

SLIGHT (MICROTONE) BEND: Strike the note and bend up 1/4 step.

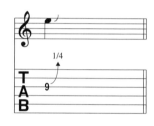

BEND AND RELEASE: Strike the note and bend up as indicated, then release back to the original note. Only the first note is struck.

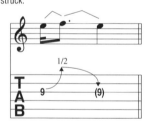

PRE-BEND: Bend the note as indicated, then strike it.

PRE-BEND AND RELEASE: Bend the note as indicated. Strike it and release the bend back to the original note.

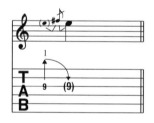

UNISON BEND: Strike the two notes simultaneously and bend the lower note up to the pitch of the higher.

VIBRATO: The string is vibrated by rapidly bending and releasing the note with the fretting hand.

WIDE VIBRATO: The pitch is varied to a greater degree by vibrating with the fretting hand.

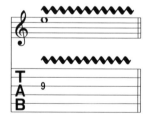

HAMMER-ON: Strike the first (lower) note with one finger, then sound the higher note (on the same string) with another finger by fretting it without picking.

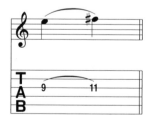

PULL-OFF: Place both fingers on the notes to be sounded. Strike the first note and without picking, pull the finger off to sound the second (lower) note.

LEGATO SLIDE: Strike the first note and then slide the same fret-hand finger up or down to the second note. The second note is not struck.

SHIFT SLIDE: Same as legato slide, except the second note is struck.

TRILL: Very rapidly alternate between the notes indicated by continuously hammering on and pulling off.

TAPPING: Hammer ("tap") the fret indicated with the pick-hand index or middle finger and pull off to the note fretted by the fret hand.

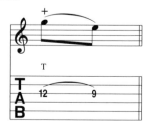

NATURAL HARMONIC: Strike the note while the fret-hand lightly touches the string directly over the fret indicated.

PINCH HARMONIC: The note is fretted normally and a harmonic is produced by adding the edge of the thumb or the tip of the index finger of the pick hand to the normal pick attack.

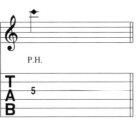

HARP HARMONIC: The note is fretted normally and a harmonic is produced by gently resting the pick hand's index finger directly above the indicated fret (in parentheses) while the pick hand's thumb or pick assists by plucking the appropriate string.

PICK SCRAPE: The edge of the pick is rubbed down (or up) the string, producing a scratchy sound.

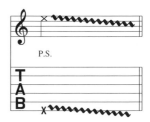

MUFFLED STRINGS: A percussive sound is produced by laying the fret hand across the string(s) without depressing, and striking them with the pick hand.

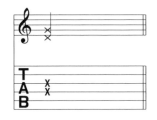

PALM MUTING: The note is partially muted by the pick hand lightly touching the string(s) just before the bridge.

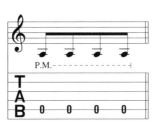

RAKE: Drag the pick across the strings indicated with a single motion.

TREMOLO PICKING: The note is picked as rapidly and continuously as possible.

ARPEGGIATE: Play the notes of the chord indicated by quickly rolling them from bottom to top.

VIBRATO BAR DIVE AND RETURN: The pitch of the note or chord is dropped a specified number of steps (in rhythm) then returned to the original pitch.

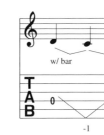

VIBRATO BAR SCOOP: Depress the bar just before striking the note, then quickly release the bar.

VIBRATO BAR DIP: Strike the note and then immediately drop a specified number of steps, then release back to the original pitch.

Additional Musical Definitions

 (accent) • Accentuate note (play it louder)

 (accent) • Accentuate note with great intensity

 (staccato) • Play the note short

⊓ • Downstroke

∨ • Upstroke

D.S. al Coda • Go back to the sign (𝄋), then play until the measure marked "***To Coda***," then skip to the section labelled "**Coda**."

D.C. al Fine • Go back to the beginning of the song and play until the measure marked "***Fine***" (end).

Rhy. Fig. • Label used to recall a recurring accompaniment pattern (usually chordal).

Riff • Label used to recall composed, melodic lines (usually single notes) which recur.

Fill • Label used to identify a brief melodic figure which is to be inserted into the arrangement.

Rhy. Fill • A chordal version of a Fill.

tacet • Instrument is silent (drops out).

 • Repeat measures between signs.

 • When a repeated section has different endings, play the first ending only the first time and the second ending only the second time.

NOTE: Tablature numbers in parentheses mean:
1. The note is being sustained over a system (note in standard notation is tied), or
2. The note is sustained, but a new articulation (such as a hammer-on, pull-off, slide or vibrato begins), or
3. The note is a barely audible "ghost" note (note in standard notation is also in parentheses).

Guitar Recorded Versions®

AUTHENTIC TRANSCRIPTIONS WITH NOTES AND TABLATURE

   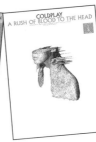